BLESSED
BEYOND
MEASURE

BLESSED
BEYOND
MEASURE

Compiled by Eugene Carvalho

Blessed Beyond Measure

Copyright © 2019 by Eugene Carvalho

ISBN - 9781543183177

Printed in the United States of America

To the Body of Christ.
May this compilation bless you richly!
With love…

TABLE OF CONTENTS

PURPOSE AND ACKNOWLEDGEMENTS

The infallible Word of God for faith and conduct informs us that the Holy Spirit gives gifts to men and women of the Body of Christ. It states: "the gifts edify the body for the building up of the saints" (Eph. 4:12). I hope the talents and gifts the Lord has given me will be a blessing to someone else through the reading of this compilation.

I am grateful for the love from all family members, especially my wife Mercedes Carvalho. I am also grateful for the knowledge, wisdom and love of many pastors, teachers, and saints that the Lord has used to bless me. Lastly, I must not forget a special thank you to my friend Kathryn Regan for proofreading this material.

Chapter One

BLESSED BEYOND MEASURE

We learn from the first chapter of the Bible that God created the very first man (Adam) in His image and then gave Adam authority over the whole earth. It is God's nature to bless. That's why God says in Malachi, "…Yet ye have robbed me…" (Mal. 3:8 KJV). When individuals do not pay tithes, they rob God of being able to bless them. His nature is to bless. He loves to bless His people, but He cannot bless rebellion.

The covenants of the Bible include Adam and Eve, Noah and the ark, Moses and the Law, David and the kingdom of Israel, and Jesus Christ and the new covenant. God intended His first covenant with man to be permanent. However, because of man's rebellion and sin, man continued to be separated from God; which is why Jesus was sent by God. Jesus is the mediator in the final covenant with mankind.

Throughout the Bible we see how God blessed His people. This book investigates the Bible verses that discuss the phrase "blessed." I want you to know, God loves you as much right now as He ever will. You just have to receive it by faith. God has already blessed you with everything you will ever need. You just have to receive it by faith, because it's a finished work. He is not going to bless you with anything else that He has not already blessed you with. You just have to receive everything by faith. The most important blessing an individual can receive from God is the forgiveness of their sins and salvation through His Son, Jesus Christ.

Before we get into the main text, I would like to look at the meaning of *bless, blessing* from a biblical perspective. "Bless, blessing – the act of declaring, or wishing, favor and goodness upon others. The blessing is not only the good effect of words; it also has the power to bring them to pass. In the Bible, important persons blessed those with less power or influence. The patriarchs pronounced benefits upon their children, often near their own deaths (Gen. 49:1-28). Even if spoken by mistake, once a blessing was given it could not be taken back (Gen. 27:33).

"Leaders often blessed people, especially when getting ready to leave them. These included Moses (Dt. 33), Joshua (22:6-7), and Jesus (Lk 24:50). Equals could bless each other by being friendly (Gen. 12:3). One can also bless God, showing gratitude to Him (Dt. 8:10) in songs of praise (Ps. 103:1-2).

"God also blesses people by giving life, riches, fruitfulness, or plenty (Gen. 1:22, 28). His greatest blessing is turning us from evil (Acts 3:25-26) and forgiving our sins (Rom. 4:7-8).

"Cases of the opposite of blessing, or cursing, are often cited in the Bible (Dt. 27:11-26). Although the natural reaction to a curse is to curse back, Christians are called to bless — to ask for the person's benefit (Matt. 5:44)."[1]

Let's study the Word and examine our topic.

---

[1] Ronald F. Youngblood, *Nelson's New Illustrated Bible Dictionary*, Nashville, Thomas Nelson, Inc. 1995, p. 220.

BLESSED IN THE OLD TESTAMENT

IN THE BOOK OF GENESIS

God Blessed Them, Saying, "Be fruitful and Multiply"

"Then God said, 'Let the waters teem with swarms of living creatures, and let birds fly above the earth in the open expanse of the heavens.' God created the great sea monsters and every living creature that moves, with which the waters swarmed after their kind, and every winged bird after its kind; and God saw that it was good. God blessed them, saying, 'Be fruitful and multiply, and fill the waters in the seas, and let birds multiply on the earth.' There was evening and there was morning, a fifth day" (Ge. 1:20-23).[2]

God Blessed Them and Said Fill the Earth, and Subdue It

"Then God said, 'Let Us make man in Our image, according to Our likeness; and let them rule over the fish of the sea and over the birds of the sky and over the cattle and over all the earth, and over every creeping thing that creeps on the earth.' God created man in His own image, in the image of God He created him; male and female He created them. God blessed them; and God said to them, 'Be fruitful and multiply, and fill the earth, and subdue it; and

---

[2] All Scripture quotations, unless otherwise noted, are from the *New American Standard Bible*.

rule over the fish of the sea and over the birds of the sky and over every living thing that moves on the earth.' Then God said, 'Behold, I have given you every plant yielding seed that is on the surface of all the earth, and every tree which has fruit yielding seed; it shall be food for you; and to every beast of the earth and to every bird of the sky and to every thing that moves on the earth which has life, I have given every green plant for food'; and it was so. God saw all that He had made, and behold, it was very good. And there was evening and there was morning, the sixth day" (Ge. 1:26-31).

God Blessed the Seventh Day and Sanctified It

"Thus the heavens and the earth were completed, and all their hosts. By the seventh day God completed His work which He had done, and He rested on the seventh day from all His work which He had done. Then God blessed the seventh day and sanctified it, because in it He rested from all His work which God had created and made" (Ge. 2:1-3).

He Created Them Male and Female, and He Blessed Them

"This is the book of the generations of Adam. In the day when God created man, He made him in the likeness of God. He created them male and female, and He blessed them and named them Man in the day when they were created" (Ge. 5:1-2).

Chapter Two

God Blessed Noah and His Sons

"And God blessed Noah and his sons and said to them, 'Be fruitful and multiply, and fill the earth. The fear of you and the terror of you will be on every beast of the earth and on every bird of the sky; with everything that creeps on the ground, and all the fish of the sea, into your hand they are given. Every moving thing that is alive shall be food for you; I give all to you, as I gave the green plant. Only you shall not eat flesh with its life, that is, its blood. Surely I will require your lifeblood; from every beast I will require it. And from every man, from every man's brother I will require the life of man. Whoever sheds man's blood, by man his blood shall be shed, for in the image of God He made man. As for you, be fruitful and multiply; populate the earth abundantly and multiply in it'" (Ge. 9:1-7).

Blessed Be the Lord, the God of Shem

"Then Noah began farming and planted a vineyard. He drank of the wine and became drunk, and uncovered himself inside his tent. Ham, the father of Canaan, saw the nakedness of his father, and told his two brothers outside. But Shem and Japheth took a garment and laid it upon both their shoulders and walked backward and covered the nakedness of their father; and their faces were turned away, so that they did not see their father's nakedness. When Noah awoke from his wine, he knew what his youngest son had done to him. So he said, 'Cursed be Canaan; A servant of servants He shall be to his brothers.' He also said, 'Blessed be the

15

Lord, the God of Shem; and let Canaan be his servant. May God enlarge Japheth, and let him dwell in the tents of Shem; and let Canaan be his servant'" (Ge. 9:20-27).

I Will Bless Those Who Bless You

"Now the Lord said to Abram, 'Go forth from your country, and from your relatives and from your father's house, To the land which I will show you; and I will make you a great nation, and I will bless you, and make your name great; and so you shall be a blessing; and I will bless those who bless you, and the one who curses you I will curse. And in you all the families of the earth will be blessed'" (Ge. 12:1-3).

Blessed Be Abram of God Most High

"Then after his return from the defeat of Chedorlaomer and the kings who were with him, the king of Sodom went out to meet him at the valley of Shaveh (that is, the King's Valley). And Melchizedek king of Salem brought out bread and wine; now he was a priest of God Most High. He blessed him and said, 'Blessed be Abram of God Most High, Possessor of heaven and earth; and blessed be God Most High, who has delivered your enemies into your hand.' He gave him a tenth of all. The king of Sodom said to Abram, 'Give the people to me and take the goods for yourself.' Abram said to the king of Sodom, 'I have sworn to the Lord God Most High, possessor of heaven and earth, that I will not take a thread or a sandal thong or anything that is yours, for fear you would say, "I have made

Abram rich." I will take nothing except what the young men have eaten, and the share of the men who went with me, Aner, Eshcol, and Mamre; let them take their share'" (Ge. 14:17-24).

In Him All the Nations of the Earth Will Be Blessed

"Then the men rose up from there, and looked down toward Sodom; and Abraham was walking with them to send them off. The Lord said, 'Shall I hide from Abraham what I am about to do, since Abraham will surely become a great and mighty nation, and in him all the nations of the earth will be blessed? For I have chosen him, so that he may command his children and his household after him to keep the way of the Lord by doing righteousness and justice, so that the Lord may bring upon Abraham what He has spoken about him.' And the Lord said, 'The outcry of Sodom and Gomorrah is indeed great, and their sin is exceedingly grave. I will go down now, and see if they have done entirely according to its outcry, which has come to Me; and if not, I will know'" (Ge. 18:16-21).

In Your Seed All the Nations of the Earth Shall Be Blessed

"Then the angel of the Lord called to Abraham a second time from heaven, and said, 'By Myself I have sworn, declares the Lord, because you have done this thing and have not withheld your son, your only son, indeed I will greatly bless you, and I will greatly multiply your seed as the stars of the heavens and as the sand which is on the seashore; and your seed shall possess the gate of their enemies. In your seed all the nations of the earth shall be blessed, because you have obeyed My voice.' So Abraham returned to his young men, and they arose and went together to Beersheba; and Abraham lived at Beersheba" (Ge. 22:15-19).

The Lord Had Blessed Abraham in Every Way

"Now Abraham was old, advanced in age; and the Lord had blessed Abraham in every way. Abraham said to his servant, the oldest of his household, who had charge of all that he owned, 'Please place your hand under my thigh, and I will make you swear by the Lord, the God of heaven and the God of earth, that you shall not take a wife for my son from the daughters of the Canaanites, among whom I live, but you will go to my country and to my relatives, and take a wife for my son Isaac.' The servant said to him, 'Suppose the woman is not willing to follow me to this land; should I take your son back to the land from where you came?' Then Abraham said to him, 'Beware that you do not take my son back there! The Lord, the God of heaven, who took me from my father's house and from the land of my birth, and who spoke to me and who swore to me, saying, "To your descendants I will give this land," He will send His angel before you, and you will take a wife for my son from there. But if the woman is not willing to follow you, then you will be free from this my oath; only do not take my son back there.' So the servant placed his hand under the thigh of Abraham his master, and swore to him concerning this matter" (Ge. 24:1-9).

Blessed the Lord, the God of My Master Abraham

"When the camels had finished drinking, the man took a gold ring weighing a half-shekel and two bracelets for her wrists weighing ten shekels in gold, and said, 'Whose daughter are you? Please tell me, is there room for us to lodge in your father's house?' She said to him, 'I am the daughter of Bethuel, the son of Milcah, whom she bore to Nahor.' Again she said to him, 'We have plenty of both straw and feed, and room to lodge in.' Then the man bowed low and worshiped the Lord. He said, 'Blessed be the Lord, the God of my master Abraham, who has not forsaken His lovingkindness and His truth toward my master; as for me, the Lord has guided me in the way to the house of my master's brothers'" (Ge. 24:22-27).

The Lord Has Greatly Blessed My Master

"Then the girl ran and told her mother's household about these things. Now Rebekah had a brother whose name was Laban; and Laban ran outside to the man at the spring. When he saw the ring and the bracelets on his sister's wrists, and when he heard the words of Rebekah his sister, saying, 'This is what the man said to me,' he went to the man; and behold, he was standing by the camels at the spring. And he said, 'Come in, blessed of the Lord! Why do you stand outside since I have prepared the house, and a place for the camels?' So the man entered the house. Then Laban unloaded the camels, and he gave straw and feed to the camels, and water to wash his feet and the feet of the men who were with him. But when food was set before him to eat, he said, 'I will not eat until I have told my business.' And he said, 'Speak on.' So he said, 'I am Abraham's servant. The Lord has greatly blessed my master, so that he has become rich; and He has given him flocks and herds, and silver and gold, and servants and maids, and camels and donkeys. Now Sarah my master's wife bore a son to my master in her old age, and he has given him all that he has. My master made me swear, saying, "You shall not take a wife for my son from the daughters of the Canaanites, in whose land I live; but you shall go to my father's house and to my relatives, and take a wife for my son." I said to my master, "Suppose the woman does not follow me." He said to me, "The Lord, before whom I have walked, will send His angel with you to make your journey successful, and you will take a wife for my son from my relatives and from my father's house; then you will be free from my oath, when you come to my relatives; and if they do not give her to you, you will be free from my oath"'" (Ge. 24:28-41).

I Bowed Low, Worshiped, and Blessed the Lord

"Before I had finished speaking in my heart, behold, Rebekah came out with her jar on her shoulder, and went down to the spring and drew, and I said to her, 'Please let me drink.' She quickly lowered her jar from her shoulder, and said, 'Drink, and I will water your camels also'; so I drank, and she watered the camels also. Then I asked her, and said, 'Whose daughter are you?' And she said, 'The daughter of Bethuel, Nahor's son, whom Milcah bore to him'; and I put the ring on her nose, and the bracelets on her wrists. And I bowed low and worshiped the Lord, and blessed the Lord, the God of my master Abraham, who had guided me in the right way to take the daughter of my master's kinsman for his son. So now if you are going to deal kindly and truly with my master, tell me; and if not, let me know, that I may turn to the right hand or the left" (Ge. 24:45-49).

They Blessed Rebekah

"When Abraham's servant heard their words, he bowed himself to the ground before the Lord. The servant brought out articles of silver and articles of gold, and garments, and gave them to Rebekah; he also gave precious things to her brother and to her mother. Then he and the men who were with him ate and drank and spent the night. When they arose in the morning, he said, 'Send me away to my master.' But her brother and her mother said, 'Let the girl stay with us a few days, say ten; afterward she may go.' He said to them, 'Do not delay me, since the Lord has prospered my way. Send me away that I may go to my master.' And they said, 'We will call the girl and consult her wishes.' Then they called Rebekah and said to her, 'Will you go with this man?' And she said, 'I will go.' Thus they sent away their sister Rebekah and her nurse with Abraham's servant and his men. They blessed Rebekah and said to her, 'May you, our sister, become thousands of ten thousands, and may your descendants possess the gate of those who hate them.' Then Rebekah arose with her maids, and they mounted the camels and followed the man. So the servant took Rebekah and departed" (Ge. 24:52-61).

God Blessed Isaac and He Lived by Beer-lahai-roi

"These are all the years of Abraham's life that he lived, one hundred and seventy-five years. Abraham breathed his last and died in a ripe old age, an old man and satisfied with life; and he was gathered to his people. Then his sons Isaac and Ishmael buried him in the cave of Machpelah, in the field of Ephron the son of Zohar the Hittite, facing Mamre, the field which Abraham purchased from the sons of Heth; there Abraham was buried with Sarah his wife. It came about after the death of Abraham, that God blessed his son Isaac; and Isaac lived by Beer-lahai-roi" (Ge. 25:7-11).

By Your Descendants All the Nations of the Earth Shall Be Blessed

"Now there was a famine in the land, besides the previous famine that had occurred in the days of Abraham. So Isaac went to Gerar, to Abimelech king of the Philistines. The Lord appeared to him and said, 'Do not go down to Egypt; stay in the land of which I shall tell you. Sojourn in this land and I will be with you and bless you, for to you and to your descendants I will give all these lands, and I will establish the oath which I swore to your father Abraham. I will multiply your descendants as the stars of heaven, and will give your descendants all these lands; and by your descendants all the nations of the earth shall be blessed; because Abraham obeyed Me and kept My charge, My commandments, My statutes and My laws"' (Ge. 26:1-5).

Isaac Sowed in that Land and the Lord Blessed Him

"Now Isaac sowed in that land and reaped in the same year a hundredfold. And the Lord blessed him, and the man became rich, and continued to grow richer until he became very wealthy; for he had possessions of flocks and herds and a great household, so that the Philistines envied him. Now all the wells which his father's servants had dug in the days of Abraham his father, the Philistines stopped up by filling them with earth. Then Abimelech said to Isaac, 'Go away from us, for you are too powerful for us.' And Isaac departed from there and camped in the valley of Gerar, and settled ther" (Ge. 26:12-17).

You Are Now the Blessed of the Lord

"Then Abimelech came to him from Gerar with his adviser Ahuzzath and Phicol the commander of his army. Isaac said to them, 'Why have you come to me, since you hate me and have sent me away from you?' They said, 'We see plainly that the Lord has been with you; so we said, "Let there now be an oath between us, even between you and us, and let us make a covenant with you, that you will do us no harm, just as we have not touched you and have done to you nothing but good and have sent you away in peace. You are now the blessed of the Lord."' Then he made them a feast, and they ate and drank. In the morning they arose early and exchanged oaths; then Isaac sent them away and they departed from him in peace. Now it came about on the same day, that Isaac's servants came in and told him about the well which they had dug, and said to him, 'We have found water.' So he called it Shibah; therefore the name of the city is Beersheba to this day" (Ge. 26:26-33).

His Hands Were Hairy so He Blessed Him

"Then he came to his father and said, 'My father.' And he said, 'Here I am. Who are you, my son?' Jacob said to his father, 'I am Esau your firstborn; I have done as you told me. Get up, please, sit and eat of my game, that you may bless me.' Isaac said to his son, 'How is it that you have it so quickly, my son?' And he said, 'Because the Lord your God caused it to happen to me.' Then Isaac said to Jacob, 'Please come close, that I may feel you, my son, whether you are really my son Esau or not.' So Jacob came close to Isaac his father, and he felt him and said, 'The voice is the voice of Jacob, but the hands are the hands of Esau.' He did not recognize him, because his hands were hairy like his brother Esau's hands; so he blessed him. And he said, 'Are you really my son Esau?' And he said, 'I am.' So he said, 'Bring it to me, and I will eat of my son's game, that I may bless you.' And he brought it to him, and he ate; he also brought him wine and he drank. Then his father Isaac said to him, 'Please come close and kiss me, my son.' So he came close and kissed him; and when he smelled the smell of his garments, he blessed him and said, 'See, the smell of my son Is like the smell of a field which the Lord has blessed; now may God give you of the dew of heaven, and of the fatness of the earth, and an abundance of grain and new wine; may peoples serve you, and nations bow down to you; be master of your brothers, and may your mother's sons bow down to you. Cursed be those who curse you, and blessed be those who bless you'" (Ge. 27:18-29).

Yes, and He Shall Be Blessed

"Now it came about, as soon as Isaac had finished blessing Jacob, and Jacob had hardly gone out from the presence of Isaac his father, that Esau his brother came in from his hunting. Then he also made savory food, and brought it to his father; and he said to his father, 'Let my father arise and eat of his son's game, that you may bless me.' Isaac his father said to him, 'Who are you?' And he said, 'I am your son, your firstborn, Esau.' Then Isaac trembled violently, and said, 'Who was he then that hunted game and brought it to me, so that I ate of all of it before you came, and blessed him? Yes, and he shall be blessed.' When Esau heard the words of his father, he cried out with an exceedingly great and bitter cry, and said to his father, 'Bless me, even me also, O my father!' And he said, 'Your brother came deceitfully and has taken away your blessing.' Then he said, 'Is he not rightly named Jacob, for he has supplanted me these two times? He took away my birthright, and behold, now he has taken away my blessing.' And he said, 'Have you not reserved a blessing for me?' But Isaac replied to Esau, 'Behold, I have made him your master, and all his relatives I have given to him as servants; and with grain and new wine I have sustained him. Now as for you then, what can I do, my son?' Esau said to his father, 'Do you have only one blessing, my father? Bless me, even me also, O my father.' So Esau lifted his voice and wept. Then Isaac his father answered and said to him, 'Behold, away from the fertility of the earth shall be your dwelling, and away from the dew of heaven from above. By your sword you shall live, and your brother you shall serve; but it shall come about when you become restless, that you will break his yoke from your neck'" (Ge. 27:30-40).

His Father Had Blessed Him

"So Esau bore a grudge against Jacob because of the blessing with which his father had blessed him; and Esau said to himself, 'The days of mourning for my father are near; then I will kill my brother Jacob.' Now when the words of her elder son Esau were reported to Rebekah, she sent and called her younger son Jacob, and said to him, 'Behold your brother Esau is consoling himself concerning you by planning to kill you. Now therefore, my son, obey my voice, and arise, flee to Haran, to my brother Laban! Stay with him a few days, until your brother's fury subsides, until your brother's anger against you subsides and he forgets what you did to him. Then I will send and get you from there. Why should I be bereaved of you both in one day'" (Ge. 27:41-45)?

Isaac Blessed Jacob and Charged Him

"So Isaac called Jacob and blessed him and charged him, and said to him, 'You shall not take a wife from the daughters of Canaan. Arise, go to Paddan-aram, to the house of Bethuel your mother's father; and from there take to yourself a wife from the daughters of Laban your mother's brother. May God Almighty bless you and make you fruitful and multiply you, that you may become a company of peoples. May He also give you the blessing of Abraham, to you and to your descendants with you, that you may possess the land of your sojournings, which God gave to Abraham.' Then Isaac sent Jacob away, and he went to Paddan-aram to Laban, son of Bethuel the Aramean, the brother of Rebekah, the mother of Jacob and Esau" (Ge. 28:1-5).

Esau Saw that Isaac Had Blessed Jacob

"Now Esau saw that Isaac had blessed Jacob and sent him away to Paddan-aram to take to himself a wife from there, and that when he blessed him he charged him, saying, 'You shall not take a wife from the daughters of Canaan,' and that Jacob had obeyed his father and his mother and had gone to Paddan-aram. So Esau saw that the daughters of Canaan displeased his father Isaac; and Esau went to Ishmael, and married, besides the wives that he had, Mahalath the daughter of Ishmael, Abraham's son, the sister of Nebaioth" (Ge. 28:6-9).

In Your Descendants Shall All the Families of the Earth be Blessed

"Then Jacob departed from Beersheba and went toward Haran. He came to a certain place and spent the night there, because the sun had set; and he took one of the stones of the place and put it under his head, and lay down in that place. He had a dream, and behold, a ladder was set on the earth with its top reaching to heaven; and behold, the angels of God were ascending and descending on it. And behold, the Lord stood above it and said, 'I am the Lord, the God of your father Abraham and the God of Isaac; the land on which you lie, I will give it to you and to your descendants. Your descendants will also be like the dust of the earth, and you will spread out to the west and to the east and to the north and to the south; and in you and in your descendants shall all the families of the earth be blessed. Behold, I am with you and will keep you wherever you go, and will bring you back to this land; for I will not leave you until I have done what I have promised you.' Then Jacob awoke from his sleep and said, 'Surely the Lord is in this place, and I did not know it.' He was afraid and said, 'How awesome is this place! This is none other than the house of God, and this is the gate of heaven'" (Ge. 28:10-17).

The Lord Has Blessed Me on Your Account

"Now it came about when Rachel had borne Joseph, that Jacob said to Laban, 'Send me away, that I may go to my own place and to my own country. Give me my wives and my children for whom I have served you, and let me depart; for you yourself know my service which I have rendered you.' But Laban said to him, 'If now it pleases you, stay with me; I have divined that the Lord has blessed me on your account.' He continued, 'Name me your wages, and I will give it.' But he said to him, 'You yourself know how I have served you and how your cattle have fared with me. For you had little before I came and it has increased to a multitude, and the Lord has blessed you wherever I turned. But now, when shall I provide for my own household also?' So he said, 'What shall I give you?' And Jacob said, 'You shall not give me anything. If you will do this one thing for me, I will again pasture and keep your flock: let me pass through your entire flock today, removing from there every speckled and spotted sheep and every black one among the lambs and the spotted and speckled among the goats; and such shall be my wages. So my honesty will answer for me later, when you come concerning my wages. Every one that is not speckled and spotted among the goats and black among the lambs, if found with me, will be considered stolen.' Laban said, 'Good, let it be according to your word.' So he removed on that day the striped and spotted male goats and all the speckled and spotted female goats, every one with white in it, and all the black ones among the sheep, and gave them into the care of his sons. And he put a distance of three days' journey between himself and Jacob, and Jacob fed the rest of Laban's flocks" (Ge. 30:25-36).

Chapter Two

Laban Blessed His Sons and Daughters

"Then Laban replied to Jacob, 'The daughters are my daughters, and the children are my children, and the flocks are my flocks, and all that you see is mine. But what can I do this day to these my daughters or to their children whom they have borne? So now come, let us make a covenant, you and I, and let it be a witness between you and me.' Then Jacob took a stone and set it up as a pillar. Jacob said to his kinsmen, 'Gather stones.' So they took stones and made a heap, and they ate there by the heap. Now Laban called it Jegar-sahadutha, but Jacob called it Galeed. Laban said, 'This heap is a witness between you and me this day.' Therefore it was named Galeed, and Mizpah, for he said, 'May the LORD watch between you and me when we are absent one from the other. If you mistreat my daughters, or if you take wives besides my daughters, although no man is with us, see, God is witness between you and me.' Laban said to Jacob, 'Behold this heap and behold the pillar which I have set between you and me. This heap is a witness, and the pillar is a witness, that I will not pass by this heap to you for harm, and you will not pass by this heap and this pillar to me, for harm. The God of Abraham and the God of Nahor, the God of their father, judge between us.' So Jacob swore by the fear of his father Isaac. Then Jacob offered a sacrifice on the mountain, and called his kinsmen to the meal; and they ate the meal and spent the night on the mountain. Early in the morning Laban arose, and kissed his sons and his daughters and blessed them.

Then Laban departed and returned to his place" (Ge. 31:43-55).

He Blessed Him There

"Now he arose that same night and took his two wives and his two maids and his eleven children, and crossed the ford of the Jabbok. He took them and sent them across the stream. And he sent across whatever he had. Then Jacob was left alone, and a man wrestled with him until daybreak. When he saw that he had not prevailed against him, he touched the socket of his thigh; so the socket of Jacob's thigh was dislocated while he wrestled with him. Then he said, 'Let me go, for the dawn is breaking.' But he said, 'I will not let you go unless you bless me.' So he said to him, 'What is your name?' And he said, 'Jacob.' He said, 'Your name shall no longer be Jacob, but Israel; for you have striven with God and with men and have prevailed.' Then Jacob asked him and said, 'Please tell me your name.' But he said, 'Why is it that you ask my name?' And he blessed him there. So Jacob named the place Peniel, for he said, 'I have seen God face to face, yet my life has been preserved.' Now the sun rose upon him just as he crossed over Penuel, and he was limping on his thigh. Therefore, to this day the sons of Israel do not eat the sinew of the hip which is on the socket of the thigh, because he touched the socket of Jacob's thigh in the sinew of the hip" (Ge. 32:22-32).

Chapter Two

God Appeared to Jacob Again and He Blessed Him

"Then God appeared to Jacob again when he came from Paddan-aram, and He blessed him. God said to him, 'Your name is Jacob; You shall no longer be called Jacob, But Israel shall be your name.' Thus He called him Israel. God also said to him, 'I am God Almighty; be fruitful and multiply; a nation and a company of nations shall come from you, and kings shall come forth from you. The land which I gave to Abraham and Isaac, I will give it to you, and I will give the land to your descendants after you.' Then God went up from him in the place where He had spoken with him. Jacob set up a pillar in the place where He had spoken with him, a pillar of stone, and he poured out a drink offering on it; he also poured oil on it. So Jacob named the place where God had spoken with him, Bethel" (Ge. 35:9-15).

Jacob Blessed Pharaoh

"Then Joseph brought his father Jacob and presented him to Pharaoh; and Jacob blessed Pharaoh. Pharaoh said to Jacob, 'How many years have you lived?' So Jacob said to Pharaoh, 'The years of my sojourning are one hundred and thirty; few and unpleasant have been the years of my life, nor have they attained the years that my fathers lived during the days of their sojourning.' And Jacob blessed Pharaoh, and went out from his presence. So Joseph settled his father and his brothers and gave them a possession in the land of Egypt, in the best of the land, in the land of Rameses, as Pharaoh had ordered. Joseph provided his father and his brothers and all his father's household with food, according to their little ones" (Ge. 47:7-12).

God Almighty Appeared to Me and Blessed Me

"Now it came about after these things that Joseph was told, 'Behold, your father is sick.' So he took his two sons Manasseh and Ephraim with him. When it was told to Jacob, 'Behold, your son Joseph has come to you,' Israel collected his strength and sat up in the bed. Then Jacob said to Joseph, 'God Almighty appeared to me at Luz in the land of Canaan and blessed me, and He said to me, 'Behold, I will make you fruitful and numerous, and I will make you a company of peoples, and will give this land to your descendants after you for an everlasting possession.' Now your two sons, who were born to you in the land of Egypt before I came to you in Egypt, are mine; Ephraim and Manasseh shall be mine, as Reuben and Simeon are. But your offspring that have been born after them shall be yours; they shall be called by the names of their brothers in their inheritance. Now as for me, when I came from Paddan, Rachel died, to my sorrow, in the land of Canaan on the journey, when there was still some distance to go to Ephrath; and I buried her there on the way to Ephrath (that is, Bethlehem)" (Ge. 48:1-7).

He Blessed Joseph

"When Israel saw Joseph's sons, he said, 'Who are these?' Joseph said to his father, 'They are my sons, whom God has given me here.' So he said, 'Bring them to me, please, that I may bless them.'

Now the eyes of Israel were so dim from age that he could not see. Then Joseph brought them close to him, and he kissed them and embraced them. Israel said to Joseph, 'I never expected to see your face, and behold, God has let me see your children as well.' Then Joseph took them from his knees, and bowed with his face to the ground. Joseph took them both, Ephraim with his right hand toward Israel's left, and Manasseh with his left hand toward Israel's right, and brought them close to him. But Israel stretched out his right hand and laid it on the head of Ephraim, who was the younger, and his left hand on Manasseh's head, crossing his hands, although Manasseh was the firstborn. He blessed Joseph, and said, 'The God before whom my fathers Abraham and Isaac walked, The God who has been my shepherd all my life to this day, the angel who has redeemed me from all evil, bless the lads; and may my name live on in them, and the names of my fathers Abraham and Isaac; and may they grow into a multitude in the midst of the earth'" (Ge. 48:8-16).

He Blessed Them that Day

"When Joseph saw that his father laid his right hand on Ephraim's head, it displeased him; and he grasped his father's hand to remove it from Ephraim's head to Manasseh's head. Joseph said to his father, 'Not so, my father, for this one is the firstborn. Place your right hand on his head.' But his father refused and said, 'I know, my son, I know; he also will become a people and he also will be great. However, his younger brother shall be greater than he, and his descendants shall become a multitude of nations.' He blessed them that day, saying, 'By you Israel will pronounce blessing, saying, 'May God make you like Ephraim and Manasseh!'" Thus he put Ephraim before Manasseh. Then Israel said to Joseph, 'Behold, I am about to die, but God will be with you, and bring you back to the land of your fathers. I give you one portion more than your brothers, which I took from the hand of the Amorite with my sword and my bow'" (Ge. 48:17-22).

He Blessed Everyone

"Joseph is a fruitful bough, a fruitful bough by a spring; its branches run over a wall. The archers bitterly attacked him, and shot at him and harassed him; but his bow remained firm, and his arms were agile, from the hands of the Mighty One of Jacob (From there is the Shepherd, the Stone of Israel), from the God of your father who helps you, and by the Almighty who blesses you with blessings of heaven above, blessings of the deep that lies beneath, blessings of the breasts and of the womb. The blessings of your father Have surpassed the blessings of my ancestors up to the utmost bound of the everlasting hills; may they be on the head of Joseph, and on the crown of the head of the one distinguished among his brothers" (Ge. 49:22-26).

IN THE BOOK OF EXODUS

Blessed Be the Lord Who Delivered You

"Then Jethro, Moses' father-in-law, came with his sons and his wife to Moses in the

wilderness where he was camped, at the mount of
God. He sent word to Moses, 'I, your father-in-law
Jethro, am coming to you with your wife and her
two sons with her.' Then Moses went out to meet his
father-in-law, and he bowed down and kissed him;
and they asked each other of their welfare and went
into the tent. Moses told his father-in-law all that the
Lord had done to Pharaoh and to the Egyptians for
Israel's sake, all the hardship that had befallen them
on the journey, and how the Lord had delivered
them. Jethro rejoiced over all the goodness which the
Lord had done to Israel, in delivering them from the
hand of the Egyptians. So Jethro said, 'Blessed be the
Lord who delivered you from the hand of the
Egyptians and from the hand of Pharaoh, and who
delivered the people from under the hand of the
Egyptians. Now I know that the Lord is greater than
all the gods; indeed, it was proven when they dealt
proudly against the people.' Then Jethro, Moses'
father-in-law, took a burnt offering and sacrifices for
God, and Aaron came with all the elders of Israel to
eat a meal with Moses' father-in-law before God"
(Ex. 18:5-12).

The Lord Blessed the Sabbath Day and Made It Holy

"Remember the sabbath day, to keep it holy.
Six days you shall labor and do all your work, but
the seventh day is a sabbath of the Lord your God; in
it you shall not do any work, you or your son or
your daughter, your male or your female servant or
your cattle or your sojourner who stays with you.
For in six days the Lord made the heavens and the

earth, the sea and all that is in them, and rested on the seventh day; therefore the Lord blessed the sabbath day and made it holy" (Ex. 20:8-11).

Moses Blessed Them

"Thus all the work of the tabernacle of the tent of meeting was completed; and the sons of Israel did according to all that the Lord had commanded Moses; so they did. They brought the tabernacle to Moses, the tent and all its furnishings: its clasps, its boards, its bars, and its pillars and its sockets; and the covering of rams' skins dyed red, and the covering of porpoise skins, and the screening veil; the ark of the testimony and its poles and the mercy seat; the table, all its utensils, and the bread of the Presence; the pure gold lampstand, with its arrangement of lamps and all its utensils, and the oil for the light; and the gold altar, and the anointing oil and the fragrant incense, and the veil for the doorway of the tent; the bronze altar and its bronze grating, its poles and all its utensils, the laver and its stand; the hangings for the court, its pillars and its sockets, and the screen for the gate of the court, its cords and its pegs and all the equipment for the service of the tabernacle, for the tent of meeting; the woven garments for ministering in the holy place and the holy garments for Aaron the priest and the garments of his sons, to minister as priests. So the sons of Israel did all the work according to all that the Lord had commanded Moses. And Moses examined all the work and behold, they had done it; just as the Lord had commanded, this they had done. So Moses blessed them" (Ex. 39:32-43).

Chapter Two

IN THE BOOK OF LEVITICUS

Aaron Lifted Up His Hands and Blessed Them

"Then Aaron lifted up his hands toward the people and blessed them, and he stepped down after making the sin offering and the burnt offering and the peace offerings. Moses and Aaron went into the tent of meeting. When they came out and blessed the people, the glory of the Lord appeared to all the people. Then fire came out from before the Lord and consumed the burnt offering and the portions of fat on the altar; and when all the people saw it, they shouted and fell on their faces" (Lv. 9:22-24).

IN THE BOOK OF NUMBERS

I Know that He Whom You Bless Is Blessed

"Now Balak the son of Zippor saw all that Israel had done to the Amorites. So Moab was in great fear because of the people, for they were numerous; and Moab was in dread of the sons of Israel. Moab said to the elders of Midian, 'Now this horde will lick up all that is around us, as the ox licks up the grass of the field.' And Balak the son of Zippor was king of Moab at that time. So he sent messengers to Balaam the son of Beor, at Pethor, which is near the River, in the land of the sons of his people, to call him, saying, 'Behold, a people came out of Egypt; behold, they cover the surface of the land, and they are living opposite me. Now, therefore, please come, curse this people for me since they are too mighty for me; perhaps I may be able to defeat them and drive them out of the land. For I know that he whom you bless is blessed, and he whom you curse is cursed"' (Nu. 22:2-6).

Don't Curse the People, for They Are Blessed

"So the elders of Moab and the elders of Midian departed with the fees for divination in their hand; and they came to Balaam and repeated Balak's words to him. He said to them, 'Spend the night here, and I will bring word back to you as the Lord may speak to me.' And the leaders of Moab stayed with Balaam. Then God came to Balaam and said, 'Who are these men with you?' Balaam said to God, 'Balak the son of Zippor, king of Moab, has sent word to me, behold, there is a people who came out of Egypt and they cover the surface of the land; now come, curse them for me; perhaps I may be able to fight against them and drive them out.' God said to Balaam, 'Do not go with them; you shall not curse the people, for they are blessed.' So Balaam arose in the morning and said to Balak's leaders, 'Go back to your land, for the Lord has refused to let me go with you.' The leaders of Moab arose and went to Balak and said, 'Balaam refused to come with us'" (Nu. 22:7-14).

You Have Actually Blessed Them

"Then Balak said to Balaam, 'What have you done to me? I took you to curse my enemies, but behold, you have actually blessed them!' He replied, 'Must I not be careful to speak what the Lord puts in my mouth'" (Nu. 23:11-12)?

Chapter Two

When He Has Blessed, Then I Cannot Revoke It

"Then Balak said to him, 'Please come with me to another place from where you may see them, although you will only see the extreme end of them and will not see all of them; and curse them for me from there.' So he took him to the field of Zophim, to the top of Pisgah, and built seven altars and offered a bull and a ram on each altar. And he said to Balak, 'Stand here beside your burnt offering while I myself meet the Lord over there.' Then the Lord met Balaam and put a word in his mouth and said, 'Return to Balak, and thus you shall speak.' He came to him, and behold, he was standing beside his burnt offering, and the leaders of Moab with him. And Balak said to him, 'What has the Lord spoken?' Then he took up his discourse and said, 'Arise, O Balak, and hear; give ear to me, O son of Zippor! God is not a man, that He should lie, nor a son of man, that He should repent; has He said, and will He not do it? Or has He spoken, and will He not make it good? Behold, I have received a command to bless; when He has blessed, then I cannot revoke it. He has not observed misfortune in Jacob; nor has He seen trouble in Israel; the Lord his God is with him, and the shout of a king is among them. God brings them out of Egypt, He is for them like the horns of the wild ox. For there is no omen against Jacob, nor is there any divination against Israel; at the proper time it shall be said to Jacob and to Israel, what God has done! Behold, a people rises like a lioness, and as a lion it lifts itself; it will not lie down until it devours the prey, and drinks the blood of the slain'" (Nu. 23:13-24).

Chapter Two

Blessed Is Everyone Who Blesses You

"When Balaam saw that it pleased the Lord to bless Israel, he did not go as at other times to seek omens but he set his face toward the wilderness. And Balaam lifted up his eyes and saw Israel camping tribe by tribe; and the Spirit of God came upon him. He took up his discourse and said, 'The oracle of Balaam the son of Beor, and the oracle of the man whose eye is opened; the oracle of him who hears the words of God, who sees the vision of the Almighty, falling down, yet having his eyes uncovered, how fair are your tents, O Jacob, Your dwellings, O Israel! Like valleys that stretch out, like gardens beside the river, like aloes planted by the Lord, like cedars beside the waters. Water will flow from his buckets, and his seed will be by many waters, and his king shall be higher than Agag, and his kingdom shall be exalted. God brings him out of Egypt, He is for him like the horns of the wild ox. He will devour the nations who are his adversaries, and will crush their bones in pieces, and shatter them with his arrows. He couches, he lies down as a lion, and as a lion, who dares rouse him? Blessed is everyone who blesses you, and cursed is everyone who curses you'" (Nu. 24:1-9).

IN THE BOOK OF DEUTERONOMY

God Has Blessed You in All that You Have Done

"Then we turned and set out for the wilderness by the way to the Red Sea, as the Lord spoke to me, and circled Mount Seir for many days.

And the Lord spoke to me, saying, 'You have circled this mountain long enough. Now turn north, and command the people, saying, "You will pass through the territory of your brothers the sons of Esau who live in Seir; and they will be afraid of you. So be very careful; do not provoke them, for I will not give you any of their land, even as little as a footstep because I have given Mount Seir to Esau as a possession. You shall buy food from them with money so that you may eat, and you shall also purchase water from them with money so that you may drink. For the Lord your God has blessed you in all that you have done; He has known your wanderings through this great wilderness. These forty years the Lord your God has been with you; you have not lacked a thing"'" (De. 2:1-7).

You Shall Be Blessed Above All Peoples

"Then it shall come about, because you listen to these judgments and keep and do them, that the Lord your God will keep with you His covenant and His lovingkindness which He swore to your forefathers. He will love you and bless you and multiply you; He will also bless the fruit of your womb and the fruit of your ground, your grain and your new wine and your oil, the increase of your herd and the young of your flock, in the land which He swore to your forefathers to give you. You shall be blessed above all peoples; there will be no male or female barren among you or among your cattle. The Lord will remove from you all sickness; and He will not put on you any of the harmful diseases of Egypt which you have known, but He will lay them on all who hate you. You shall consume all the peoples whom the Lord your God will deliver to you; your eye shall not pity them, nor shall you serve their gods, for that would be a snare to you" (Dt. 7:12-16).

Your God Has Blessed You

"These are the statutes and the judgments which you shall carefully observe in the land which the Lord, the God of your fathers, has given you to possess as long as you live on the earth. You shall utterly destroy all the places where the nations whom you shall dispossess serve their gods, on the high mountains and on the hills and under every green tree. You shall tear down their altars and smash their sacred pillars and burn their Asherim with fire, and you shall cut down the engraved images of their gods and obliterate their name from that place. You shall not act like this toward the Lord your God. But you shall seek the Lord at the place which the Lord your God will choose from all your tribes, to establish His name there for His dwelling, and there you shall come. There you shall bring your burnt offerings, your sacrifices, your tithes, the contribution of your hand, your votive offerings, your freewill offerings, and the firstborn of your herd and of your flock. There also you and your households shall eat before the Lord your God, and rejoice in all your undertakings in which the Lord your God has blessed you" (Dt. 12:1-7).

Give to Him as the Lord Has Blessed You

"If your kinsman, a Hebrew man or woman, is sold to you, then he shall serve you six years, but in the seventh year you shall set him free. When you set him free, you shall not send him away empty-handed. You shall furnish him liberally from your flock and from your threshing floor and from your wine vat; you shall give to him as the Lord your God has blessed you. You shall remember that you were a slave in the land of Egypt, and the Lord your God redeemed you; therefore I command you this today. It shall come about if he says to you, 'I will not go out from you,' because he loves you and your household, since he fares well with you; then you shall take an awl and pierce it through his ear into the door, and he shall be your servant forever. Also you shall do likewise to your maidservant" (Dt. 15:12-17).

Blessed Shall You Be

"Blessed shall you be in the city, and blessed shall you be in the country. Blessed shall be the offspring of your body and the produce of your ground and the offspring of your beasts, the increase of your herd and the young of your flock. Blessed shall be your basket and your kneading bowl. Blessed shall you be when you come in, and blessed shall you be when you go out" (Dt .28:3-6).

Chapter Two

Moses the Man of God Blessed the Sons of Israel

"Now this is the blessing with which Moses the man of God blessed the sons of Israel before his death. He said, 'The Lord came from Sinai, and dawned on them from Seir; He shone forth from Mount Paran, and He came from the midst of ten thousand holy ones; at His right hand there was flashing lightning for them. Indeed, He loves the people; all Your holy ones are in Your hand, and they followed in Your steps; everyone receives of Your words. Moses charged us with a law, a possession for the assembly of Jacob. And He was king in Jeshurun, when the heads of the people were gathered, the tribes of Israel together'" (Dt. 33:1-5).

Blessed of the Lord Be His Land

"Of Joseph he said, 'Blessed of the Lord be his land, with the choice things of heaven, with the dew, and from the deep lying beneath, and with the choice yield of the sun, and with the choice produce of the months. And with the best things of the ancient mountains, and with the choice things of the everlasting hills, and with the choice things of the earth and its fullness, and the favor of Him who dwelt in the bush. Let it come to the head of Joseph, and to the crown of the head of the one distinguished among his brothers. As the firstborn of his ox, majesty is his, and his horns are the horns of the wild ox; with them he will push the peoples, all at once, to the ends of the earth. And those are the ten thousands of Ephraim, and those are the thousands of Manasseh'" (Dt. 33:13-17).

Chapter Two

Blessed Is the One Who Enlarges Gad

"Of Gad he said, 'Blessed is the one who enlarges Gad; he lies down as a lion, and tears the arm, also the crown of the head. Then he provided the first part for himself, for there the ruler's portion was reserved; and he came with the leaders of the people; he executed the justice of the Lord, and His ordinances with Israel'" (Dt. 33:20-21).

More Blessed than Sons Is Asher

"Of Asher he said, 'More blessed than sons is Asher; may he be favored by his brothers, and may he dip his foot in oil. Your locks will be iron and bronze, and according to your days, so will your leisurely walk be'" (Dt. 33:24-25).

Blessed Are You, O Israel

"There is none like the God of Jeshurun, who rides the heavens to your help, and through the skies in His majesty. The eternal God is a dwelling place, and underneath are the everlasting arms; and He drove out the enemy from before you, and said, 'Destroy!' So Israel dwells in security, the fountain of Jacob secluded, in a land of grain and new wine; His heavens also drop down dew. Blessed are you, O Israel; who is like you, a people saved by the Lord, who is the shield of your help and the sword of your majesty! So your enemies will cringe before you, and you will tread upon their high places" (Dt. 33:26-29).

Chapter Two

IN THE BOOK OF JOSHUA

Joshua Blessed Him and Gave Hebron to Caleb

"So Joshua blessed him and gave Hebron to Caleb the son of Jephunneh for an inheritance. Therefore, Hebron became the inheritance of Caleb the son of Jephunneh the Kenizzite until this day, because he followed the Lord God of Israel fully. Now the name of Hebron was formerly Kiriath-arba; for Arba was the greatest man among the Anakim. Then the land had rest from war" (Jos. 14:13-15).

People Whom the Lord Has Thus Far Blessed

"Then the sons of Joseph spoke to Joshua, saying, 'Why have you given me only one lot and one portion for an inheritance, since I am a numerous people whom the Lord has thus far blessed?' Joshua said to them, 'If you are a numerous people, go up to the forest and clear a place for yourself there in the land of the Perizzites and of the Rephaim, since the hill country of Ephraim is too narrow for you.' The sons of Joseph said, 'The hill country is not enough for us, and all the Canaanites who live in the valley land have chariots of iron, both those who are in Beth-shean and its towns and those who are in the valley of Jezreel.' Joshua spoke to the house of Joseph, to Ephraim and Manasseh, saying, 'You are a numerous people and have great power; you shall not have one lot only, but the hill country shall be yours. For though it is a forest, you shall clear it, and to its farthest borders it shall be yours; for you shall drive out the Canaanites, even though they have chariots of iron and though they are strong'" (Jos. 17:14-18).

Joshua Blessed Them and Sent Them Away

"Then Joshua summoned the Reubenites and the Gadites and the half-tribe of Manasseh, and said to them, 'You have kept all that Moses the servant of the Lord commanded you, and have listened to my voice in all that I commanded you. You have not forsaken your brothers these many days to this day, but have kept the charge of the commandment of the Lord your God. And now the Lord your God has given rest to your brothers, as He spoke to them; therefore turn now and go to your tents, to the land of your possession, which Moses the servant of the Lord gave you beyond the Jordan. Only be very careful to observe the commandment and the law which Moses the servant of the Lord commanded you, to love the Lord your God and walk in all His ways and keep His commandments and hold fast to Him and serve Him with all your heart and with all your soul.' So Joshua blessed them and sent them away, and they went to their tents" (Jos. 22:1-6).

The Sons of Israel Blessed God

"Then Phinehas the son of Eleazar the priest and the leaders returned from the sons of Reuben and from the sons of Gad, from the land of Gilead to the land of Canaan, to the sons of Israel, and brought back word to them. The word pleased the sons of Israel, and the sons of Israel blessed God; and they did not speak of going up against them in war to destroy the land in which the sons of Reuben and the sons of Gad were living. The sons of Reuben and the sons of Gad called the altar Witness; 'For,' they said, 'it is a witness between us that the Lord is God'" (Jos. 22:32-34).

IN THE BOOK OF JUDGES

Most Blessed of Women Is Jael

"Most blessed of women is Jael, the wife of Heber the Kenite; most blessed is she of women in the tent. He asked for water and she gave him milk; In a magnificent bowl she brought him curds. She reached out her hand for the tent peg, and her right hand for the workmen's hammer. Then she struck Sisera, she smashed his head; and she shattered and pierced his temple. Between her feet he bowed, he fell, he lay; between her feet he bowed, he fell; where he bowed, there he fell dead" (Jdg. 5:24-27).

The Child Grew up and the Lord Blessed Him

"Then the woman gave birth to a son and named him Samson; and the child grew up and the Lord blessed him. And the Spirit of the Lord began to stir him in Mahaneh-dan, between Zorah and Eshtaol" (Jdg. 13:24-25).

Blessed Be My Son by the Lord

"Now there was a man of the hill country of Ephraim whose name was Micah. He said to his mother, 'The eleven hundred pieces of silver which were taken from you, about which you uttered a curse in my hearing, behold, the silver is with me; I took it.' And his mother said, 'Blessed be my son by the Lord.' He then returned the eleven hundred pieces of silver to his mother, and his mother said, 'I wholly dedicate the silver from my hand to the Lord for my son to make a graven image and a molten image; now therefore, I will return them to you.' So when he returned the silver to his mother, his mother took two hundred pieces of silver and gave them to the silversmith who made them into a graven image and a molten image, and they were in the house of Micah. And the man Micah had a shrine and he made an ephod and household idols and consecrated one of his sons, that he might become his priest. In those days there was no king in Israel; every man did what was right in his own eyes" (Jdg. 17:1-6).

IN THE BOOK OF RUTH

May He Who Took Notice of You Be Blessed

"So she gleaned in the field until evening. Then she beat out what she had gleaned, and it was about an ephah of barley. She took it up and went into the city, and her mother-in-law saw what she had gleaned. She also took it out and gave Naomi what she had left after she was satisfied. Her mother-in-law then said to her, 'Where did you glean today and where did you work? May he who took notice of you be blessed.' So she told her mother-in-law with whom she had worked and said,

'The name of the man with whom I worked today is Boaz.' Naomi said to her daughter-in-law, 'May he be blessed of the Lord who has not withdrawn his kindness to the living and to the dead.' Again Naomi said to her, 'The man is our relative, he is one of our closest relatives.' Then Ruth the Moabitess said, 'Furthermore, he said to me, 'You should stay close to my servants until they have finished all my harvest.' Naomi said to Ruth her daughter-in-law, 'It is good, my daughter, that you go out with his maids, so that others do not fall upon you in another field.' So she stayed close by the maids of Boaz in order to glean until the end of the barley harvest and the wheat harvest. And she lived with her mother-in-law" (Ru. 2:17-23).

May You Be Blessed of the Lord, My Daughter

"So she went down to the threshing floor and did according to all that her mother-in-law had commanded her. When Boaz had eaten and drunk and his heart was merry, he went to lie down at the end of the heap of grain; and she came secretly, and uncovered his feet and lay down. It happened in the middle of the night that the man was startled and bent forward; and behold, a woman was lying at his feet. He said, 'Who are you?' And she answered, 'I am Ruth your maid. So spread your covering over your maid, for you are a close relative.' Then he said, 'May you be blessed of the Lord, my daughter. You have shown your last kindness to be better than the first by not going after young men, whether poor or rich. Now, my daughter, do not fear. I will do for you whatever you ask, for all my people in the city know that you are a woman of excellence. Now it is true I am a close relative; however, there is a relative closer than I. Remain this night, and when morning comes, if he will redeem you, good; let him redeem you. But if he does not wish to redeem you, then I will redeem you, as the Lord lives. Lie down until morning'" (Ru. 3:6-13).

Blessed Is the Lord Who Has Not Left You Without a Redeemer

"So Boaz took Ruth, and she became his wife, and he went in to her. And the Lord enabled her to conceive, and she gave birth to a son. Then the women said to Naomi, 'Blessed is the Lord who has not left you without a redeemer today, and may his name become famous in Israel. May he also be to you a restorer of life and a sustainer of your old age; for your daughter-in-law, who loves you and is better to you than seven sons, has given birth to him.' Then Naomi took the child and laid him in her lap, and became his nurse. The neighbor women gave him a name, saying, 'A son has been born to Naomi!' So they named him Obed. He is the father of Jesse, the father of David" (Ru. 4:13-17).

IN THE BOOK OF 1 SAMUEL

Blessed Are You of the Lord

"Then the word of the Lord came to Samuel, saying, 'I regret that I have made Saul king, for he has turned back from following Me and has not carried out My commands.' And Samuel was distressed and cried out to the Lord all night. Samuel rose early in the morning to meet Saul; and it was told Samuel, saying, 'Saul came to Carmel, and behold, he set up a monument for himself, then turned and proceeded on down to Gilgal.' Samuel came to Saul, and Saul said to him, 'Blessed are you of the Lord! I have carried out the command of the Lord.' But Samuel said, 'What then is this bleating of the sheep in my ears, and the lowing of the oxen which I hear?' Saul said, 'They have brought them from the Amalekites, for the people spared the best of the sheep and oxen, to sacrifice to the Lord your God; but the rest we have utterly destroyed.' Then Samuel said to Saul, 'Wait, and let me tell you what the Lord said to me last night.' And he said to him, 'Speak'" (1Sa. 15:10-16)!

May You Be Blessed of the Lord, for You Have Had Compassion on Me

"Then Ziphites came up to Saul at Gibeah, saying, 'Is David not hiding with us in the strongholds at Horesh, on the hill of Hachilah, which is on the south of Jeshimon? Now then, O king, come down according to all the desire of your soul to do so; and our part shall be to surrender him into the king's hand.' Saul said, 'May you be blessed of the Lord, for you have had compassion on me. Go now, make more sure, and investigate and see his place where his haunt is, and who has seen him there; for I am told that he is very cunning. So look, and learn about all the hiding places where he hides himself and return to me with certainty, and I will go with you; and if he is in the land, I will search him out among all the thousands of Judah'" (1Sa. 23:19-23).

Blessed Be the Lord God of Israel

"Then David said to Abigail, 'Blessed be the Lord God of Israel, who sent you this day to meet me, and blessed be your discernment, and blessed be you, who have kept me this day from bloodshed and from avenging myself by my own hand. Nevertheless, as the Lord God of Israel lives, who has restrained me from harming you, unless you had come quickly to meet me, surely there would not have been left to Nabal until the morning light as much as one male.' So David received from her hand what she had brought him and said to her, 'Go up to your house in peace. See, I have listened to you and granted your request'" (1Sa. 25:32-35).

Blessed Be the Lord, Who Has Pleaded the Cause of My Reproach

"When David heard that Nabal was dead, he said, 'Blessed be the Lord, who has pleaded the cause of my reproach from the hand of Nabal and has kept back His servant from evil. The Lord has also returned the evildoing of Nabal on his own head.' Then David sent a proposal to Abigail, to take her as his wife. When the servants of David came to Abigail at Carmel, they spoke to her, saying, 'David has sent us to you to take you as his wife.' She arose and bowed with her face to the ground and said, 'Behold, your maidservant is a maid to wash the feet of my lord's servants.' Then Abigail quickly arose, and rode on a donkey, with her five maidens who attended her; and she followed the messengers of David and became his wife" (1Sa. 25:39-42).

Blessed Are You, My Son David

"Then Saul said, 'I have sinned. Return, my son David, for I will not harm you again because my life was precious in your sight this day. Behold, I have played the fool and have committed a serious error.' David replied, 'Behold the spear of the king! Now let one of the young men come over and take it. The Lord will repay each man for his righteousness and his faithfulness; for the Lord delivered you into my hand today, but I refused to stretch out my hand against the Lord's anointed. Now behold, as your life was highly valued in my sight this day, so may my life be highly valued in the sight of the Lord, and may He deliver me from all distress.' Then Saul said to David, 'Blessed are you, my son David; you will both accomplish much and surely prevail.' So David went on his way, and Saul returned to his place" (1Sa. 26:21-25).

IN THE BOOK OF 2 SAMUEL

Be Blessed of the Lord for Your Kindness

"Then it came about afterwards that David inquired of the Lord, saying, 'Shall I go up to one of the cities of Judah?' And the Lord said to him, 'Go up.' So David said, 'Where shall I go up?' And He said, 'To Hebron.' David went up there, and his two wives also, Ahinoam the Jezreelitess and Abigail the widow of Nabal the Carmelite. And David brought up his men who were with him, each with his household; and they lived in the cities of Hebron. Then the men of Judah came and there anointed David king over the house of Judah. And they told David, saying, 'It was the men of Jabesh-gilead who buried Saul.' David sent messengers to the men of Jabesh-gilead, and said to them, 'May you be blessed of the Lord because you have shown this kindness to Saul your lord, and have buried him. Now may the Lord show lovingkindness and truth to you; and I also will show this goodness to you, because you have done this thing. Now therefore, let your hands be strong and be valiant; for Saul your lord is dead, and also the house of Judah has anointed me king over them"' (2Sa. 2:1-7).

The Lord Blessed Obed-edom and All His Household

"But when they came to the threshing floor of Nacon, Uzzah reached out toward the ark of God and took hold of it, for the oxen nearly upset it. And the anger of the Lord burned against Uzzah, and God struck him down there for his irreverence; and he died there by the ark of God. David became angry because of the Lord's outburst against Uzzah, and that place is called Perez-uzzah to this day. So David was afraid of the Lord that day; and he said, 'How can the ark of the Lord come to me?' And David was unwilling to move the ark of the Lord into the city of David with him; but David took it aside to the house of Obed-edom the Gittite. Thus the ark of the Lord remained in the house of Obed-edom the Gittite three months, and the Lord blessed Obed-edom and all his household" (2Sa. 6:6-11).

They Told King David the Lord Blessed Obed-edom

"Now it was told King David, saying, 'The Lord has blessed the house of Obed-edom and all that belongs to him, on account of the ark of God.' David went and brought up the ark of God from the house of Obed-edom into the city of David with gladness. And so it was, that when the bearers of the ark of the Lord had gone six paces, he sacrificed an ox and a fatling. And David was dancing before the Lord with all his might, and David was wearing a linen ephod. So David and all the house of Israel were bringing up the ark of the Lord with shouting and the sound of the trumpet" (2Sa. 6:12-15).

He Blessed the People in the Name of the Lord

"So they brought in the ark of the Lord and set it in its place inside the tent which David had pitched for it; and David offered burnt offerings and peace offerings before the Lord. When David had finished offering the burnt offering and the peace offering, he blessed the people in the name of the Lord of hosts. Further, he distributed to all the people, to all the multitude of Israel, both to men and women, a cake of bread and one of dates and one of raisins to each one. Then all the people departed each to his house" (2Sa. 6:17-19).

Chapter Two

May the House of Your Servant Be Blessed Forever

"Then David the king went in and sat before the Lord, and he said, 'Who am I, O Lord God, and what is my house, that You have brought me this far? And yet this was insignificant in Your eyes, O Lord God, for You have spoken also of the house of Your servant concerning the distant future. And this is the custom of man, O Lord God. Again what more can David say to You? For You know Your servant, O Lord God! For the sake of Your word, and according to Your own heart, You have done all this greatness to let Your servant know. For this reason You are great, O Lord God; for there is none like You, and there is no God besides You, according to all that we have heard with our ears. And what one nation on the earth is like Your people Israel, whom God went to redeem for Himself as a people and to make a name for Himself, and to do a great thing for You and awesome things for Your land, before Your people whom You have redeemed for Yourself from Egypt, from nations and their gods? For You have established for Yourself Your people Israel as Your own people forever, and You, O Lord, have become their God. Now therefore, O Lord God, the word that You have spoken concerning Your servant and his house, confirm it forever, and do as You have spoken, that Your name may be magnified forever, by saying, "The Lord of hosts is God over Israel"; and may the house of Your servant David be established before You. For You, O Lord of hosts, the God of Israel, have made a revelation to Your servant, saying, "I will build you a house"; therefore Your servant has found courage to pray this prayer to You. Now, O Lord God, You are God, and Your words are truth, and You have promised this good thing to Your servant. Now therefore, may it please You to bless the house of Your servant, that it may continue forever before You. For You, O Lord God, have spoken; and with Your blessing may the house of Your servant be blessed forever'" (2Sa. 7:18-29).

Blessed Him

"Now it came about after two full years that Absalom had sheepshearers in Baal-hazor, which is near Ephraim, and Absalom invited all the king's sons. Absalom came to the king and said, 'Behold now, your servant has sheepshearers; please let the king and his servants go with your servant.' But the king said to Absalom, 'No, my son, we should not all go, for we will be burdensome to you.' Although he urged him, he would not go, but blessed him. Then Absalom said, 'If not, please let my brother Amnon go with us.' And the king said to him, 'Why should he go with you?' But when Absalom urged him, he let Amnon and all the king's sons go with him" (2Sa. 13:23-27).

Fell on His Face, Prostrated Himself and Blessed the King

"Then the king said to Joab, 'Behold now, I will surely do this thing; go therefore, bring back the young man Absalom.' Joab fell on his face to the ground, prostrated himself and blessed the king; then Joab said, 'Today your servant knows that I have found favor in your sight, O my lord, the king, in that the king has performed the request of his servant.' So Joab arose and went to Geshur and brought Absalom to Jerusalem. However the king said, 'Let him turn to his own house, and let him not see my face.' So Absalom turned to his own house and did not see the king's face" (2Sa. 14:21-24).

Blessed Is the Lord Your God

"Ahimaaz called and said to the king, 'All is well.' And he prostrated himself before the king with his face to the ground. And he said, 'Blessed is the Lord your God, who has delivered up the men who lifted their hands against my lord the king.' The king said, 'Is it well with the young man Absalom?' And Ahimaaz answered, 'When Joab sent the king's servant, and your servant, I saw a great tumult, but I did not know what it was.' Then the king said, 'Turn aside and stand here.' So he turned aside and stood still" (2Sa. 18:28-30).

The King Kissed Barzillai and Blessed Him

"Now Barzillai the Gileadite had come down from Rogelim; and he went on to the Jordan with the king to escort him over the Jordan. Now Barzillai was very old, being eighty years old; and he had sustained the king while he stayed at Mahanaim, for he was a very great man. The king said to Barzillai, 'You cross over with me and I will sustain you in Jerusalem with me.' But Barzillai said to the king, 'How long have I yet to live, that I should go up with the king to Jerusalem? I am now eighty years old. Can I distinguish between good and bad? Or can your servant taste what I eat or what I drink? Or can I hear anymore the voice of singing men and women? Why then should your servant be an added burden to my lord the king? Your servant would merely cross over the Jordan with the king. Why should the king compensate me with this reward? Please let your servant return, that I may die in my own city near the grave of my father and my mother. However, here is your servant Chimham, let him cross over with my lord the king, and do for him what is good in your sight.' The king answered, 'Chimham shall cross over with me, and I will do for him what is good in your sight; and whatever you require of me, I will do for you.' All the people crossed over the Jordan and the king crossed too. The king then kissed Barzillai and blessed him, and he returned to his place" (2Sa. 19:31-39).

Blessed Be My Rock

"The Lord lives, and blessed be my rock; and exalted be God, the rock of my salvation" (2Sa. 22:47).

IN THE BOOK OF 1 KINGS

Blessed Be the Lord, the God of Israel

"Now Adonijah and all the guests who were with him heard it as they finished eating. When Joab heard the sound of the trumpet, he said, 'Why is the city making such an uproar?' While he was still speaking, behold, Jonathan the son of Abiathar the priest came. Then Adonijah said, 'Come in, for you are a valiant man and bring good news.' But Jonathan replied to Adonijah, 'No! Our lord King David has made Solomon king. The king has also sent with him Zadok the priest, Nathan the prophet, Benaiah the son of Jehoiada, the Cherethites, and the Pelethites; and they have made him ride on the king's mule. Zadok the priest and Nathan the prophet have anointed him king in Gihon, and they have come up from there rejoicing, so that the city is in an uproar. This is the noise which you have heard. Besides, Solomon has even taken his seat on the throne of the kingdom. Moreover, the king's servants came to bless our lord King David, saying, "May your God make the name of Solomon better than your name and his throne greater than your throne!" And the king bowed himself on the bed. The king has also said thus, "Blessed be the Lord, the God of Israel, who has granted one to sit on my throne today while my own eyes see it"'" (1Ki. 1:41-48).

King Solomon Shall Be Blessed

"But it came about at the end of three years, that two of the servants of Shimei ran away to Achish son of Maacah, king of Gath. And they told Shimei, saying, 'Behold, your servants are in Gath.' Then Shimei arose and saddled his donkey, and went to Gath to Achish to look for his servants. And Shimei went and brought his servants from Gath. It was told Solomon that Shimei had gone from Jerusalem to Gath, and had returned. So the king sent and called for Shimei and said to him, 'Did I not make you swear by the Lord and solemnly warn you, saying, "You will know for certain that on the day you depart and go anywhere, you shall surely die"? And you said to me, "The word which I have heard is good." Why then have you not kept the oath of the Lord, and the command which I have laid on you?' The king also said to Shimei, 'You know all the evil which you acknowledge in your heart, which you did to my father David; therefore the Lord shall return your evil on your own head. But King Solomon shall be blessed, and the throne of David shall be established before the Lord forever.' So the king commanded Benaiah the son of Jehoiada, and he went out and fell upon him so that he died. Thus the kingdom was established in the hands of Solomon" (1Ki. 2:39-46).

Blessed Be the Lord Today

"When Hiram heard the words of Solomon, he rejoiced greatly and said, 'Blessed be the Lord today, who has given to David a wise son over this great people.' So Hiram sent word to Solomon, saying, 'I have heard the message which you have sent me; I will do what you desire concerning the cedar and cypress timber. My servants will bring them down from Lebanon to the sea; and I will make them into rafts to go by sea to the place where you direct me, and I will have them broken up there, and you shall carry them away. Then you shall accomplish my desire by giving food to my household.' So Hiram gave Solomon as much as he desired of the cedar and cypress timber. Solomon then gave Hiram 20,000 kors of wheat as food for his household, and twenty kors of beaten oil; thus

Solomon would give Hiram year by year. The Lord gave wisdom to Solomon, just as He promised him; and there was peace between Hiram and Solomon, and the two of them made a covenant" (1Ki. 5:7-12).

The King Blessed All the Assembly of Israel

"Then the king faced about and blessed all the assembly of Israel, while all the assembly of Israel was standing. He said, 'Blessed be the Lord, the God of Israel, who spoke with His mouth to my father David and has fulfilled it with His hand, saying, "Since the day that I brought My people Israel from Egypt, I did not choose a city out of all the tribes of Israel in which to build a house that My name might be there, but I chose David to be over My people Israel." Now it was in the heart of my father David to build a house for the name of the Lord, the God of Israel. But the Lord said to my father David, "Because it was in your heart to build a house for My name, you did well that it was in your heart. Nevertheless you shall not build the house, but your son who will be born to you, he will build the house for My name." Now the Lord has fulfilled His word which He spoke; for I have risen in place of my father David and sit on the throne of Israel, as the Lord promised, and have built the house for the name of the Lord, the God of Israel. There I have set a place for the ark, in which is the covenant of the Lord, which He made with our fathers when He brought them from the land of Egypt'" (1Ki. 8:14-21).

Chapter Two

He Stood and Blessed Everyone

"When Solomon had finished praying this entire prayer and supplication to the Lord, he arose from before the altar of the Lord, from kneeling on his knees with his hands spread toward heaven. And he stood and blessed all the assembly of Israel with a loud voice, saying: 'Blessed be the Lord, who has given rest to His people Israel, according to all that He promised; not one word has failed of all His good promise, which He promised through Moses His servant. May the Lord our God be with us, as He was with our fathers; may He not leave us or forsake us, that He may incline our hearts to Himself, to walk in all His ways and to keep His commandments and His statutes and His ordinances, which He commanded our fathers. And may these words of mine, with which I have made supplication before the Lord, be near to the Lord our God day and night, that He may maintain the cause of His servant and the cause of His people Israel, as each day requires, so that all the peoples of the earth may know that the Lord is God; there is no one else. Let your heart therefore be wholly devoted to the Lord our God, to walk in His statutes and to keep His commandments, as at this day'" (1Ki. 8:54-61).

They Blessed the King

"So Solomon observed the feast at that time, and all Israel with him, a great assembly from the entrance of Hamath to the brook of Egypt, before the Lord our God, for seven days and seven more days, even fourteen days. On the eighth day he sent the people away and they blessed the king. Then they went to their tents joyful and glad of heart for all the goodness that the Lord had shown to David His servant and to Israel His people" (1Ki. 8:65-66).

How Blessed Are They that Hear Your Wisdom

"Now when the queen of Sheba heard about the fame of Solomon concerning the name of the Lord, she came to test him with difficult questions. So she came to Jerusalem with a very large retinue, with camels carrying spices and very much gold and precious stones. When she came to Solomon, she spoke with him about all that was in her heart. Solomon answered all her questions; nothing was hidden from the king which he did not explain to her. When the queen of Sheba perceived all the wisdom of Solomon, the house that he had built, the food of his table, the seating of his servants, the attendance of his waiters and their attire, his cupbearers, and his stairway by which he went up to the house of the Lord, there was no more spirit in her. Then she said to the king, 'It was a true report which I heard in my own land about your words and your wisdom. Nevertheless I did not believe the reports, until I came and my eyes had seen it. And behold, the half was not told me. You exceed in wisdom and prosperity the report which I heard. How blessed are your men, how blessed are these your servants who stand before you continually and hear your wisdom. Blessed be the Lord your God who delighted in you to set you on the throne of Israel; because the Lord loved Israel forever, therefore He made you king, to do justice and righteousness.' She gave the king a hundred and twenty talents of gold, and a very great amount of spices and precious stones. Never again did such abundance of spices come in as that which the queen of Sheba gave King Solomon" (1Ki. 10:1-10).

IN THE BOOK OF 1 CHRONICLES

The Lord Blessed Them with All that He Had

"David and all Israel were celebrating before God with all their might, even with songs and with lyres, harps, tambourines, cymbals and with trumpets. When they came to the threshing floor of Chidon, Uzza put out his hand to hold the ark, because the oxen nearly upset it. The anger of the Lord burned against Uzza, so He struck him down because he put out his hand to the ark; and he died there before God. Then David became angry because of the Lord's outburst against Uzza; and he called that place Perez-uzza to this day. David was afraid of God that day, saying, 'How can I bring the ark of God home to me?' So David did not take the ark with him to the city of David, but took it aside to the house of Obed-edom the Gittite. Thus the ark of God remained with the family of Obed-edom in his house three months; and the Lord blessed the family of Obed-edom with all that he had" (1Ch. 13:8-14).

David Blessed the People in the Name of the Lord

"And they brought in the ark of God and placed it inside the tent which David had pitched for it, and they offered burnt offerings and peace offerings before God. When David had finished offering the burnt offering and the peace offerings, he blessed the people in the name of the Lord. He distributed to everyone of Israel, both man and woman, to everyone a loaf of bread and a portion of meat and a raisin cake" (1Ch. 16:1-3).

For You, O Lord, Have Blessed

"Now, O Lord, let the word that You have spoken concerning Your servant and concerning his house be established forever, and do as You have spoken. Let Your name be established and magnified forever, saying, 'The Lord of hosts is the God of Israel, even a God to Israel; and the house of David Your servant is established before You.' For You, O my God, have revealed to Your servant that You will build for him a house; therefore Your servant has found courage to pray before You. Now, O Lord, You are God, and have promised this good thing to Your servant. And now it has pleased You to bless the house of Your servant, that it may continue forever before You; for You, O Lord, have blessed, and it is blessed forever" (1Ch. 17:23-27).

God Had Indeed Blessed Him

"For the divisions of the gatekeepers there were of the Korahites, Meshelemiah the son of Kore, of the sons of Asaph. Meshelemiah had sons: Zechariah the firstborn, Jediael the second, Zebadiah the third, Jathniel the fourth, Elam the fifth, Johanan the sixth, Eliehoenai the seventh. Obed-edom had sons: Shemaiah the firstborn, Jehozabad the second,

Joah the third, Sacar the fourth, Nethanel the fifth, Ammiel the sixth, Issachar the seventh and Peullethai the eighth; God had indeed blessed him. Also to his son Shemaiah sons were born who ruled over the house of their father, for they were mighty men of valor. The sons of Shemaiah were Othni, Rephael, Obed and Elzabad, whose brothers, Elihu and Semachiah, were valiant men. All these were of the sons of Obed-edom; they and their sons and their relatives were able men with strength for the service, 62 from Obed-edom. Meshelemiah had sons and relatives, 18 valiant men. Also Hosah, one of the sons of Merari had sons: Shimri the first (although he was not the firstborn, his father made him first), Hilkiah the second, Tebaliah the third, Zechariah the fourth; all the sons and relatives of Hosah were 13" (1Ch. 26:1-11).

Blessed Are You, O Lord God of Israel

"So David blessed the Lord in the sight of all the assembly; and David said, 'Blessed are You, O Lord God of Israel our father, forever and ever. Yours, O Lord, is the greatness and the power and the glory and the victory and the majesty, indeed everything that is in the heavens and the earth; Yours is the dominion, O Lord, and You exalt Yourself as head over all. Both riches and honor come from You, and You rule over all, and in Your hand is power and might; and it lies in Your hand to make great and to strengthen everyone. Now therefore, our God, we thank You, and praise Your glorious name'" (1Ch. 29:10-13).

Chapter Two

They Bowed Low, Did Homage and Blessed the Lord

"Then David said to all the assembly, 'Now bless the Lord your God.' And all the assembly blessed the Lord, the God of their fathers, and bowed low and did homage to the Lord and to the king. On the next day they made sacrifices to the Lord and offered burnt offerings to the Lord, 1,000 bulls, 1,000 rams and 1,000 lambs, with their drink offerings and sacrifices in abundance for all Israel. So they ate and drank that day before the Lord with great gladness. And they made Solomon the son of David king a second time, and they anointed him as ruler for the Lord and Zadok as priest. Then Solomon sat on the throne of the Lord as king instead of David his father; and he prospered, and all Israel obeyed him. All the officials, the mighty men, and also all the sons of King David pledged allegiance to King Solomon. The Lord highly exalted Solomon in the sight of all Israel, and bestowed on him royal majesty which had not been on any king before him in Israel" (1Ch. 29:20-25).

IN THE BOOK OF 2 CHRONICLES

Blessed Be the Lord

"Then Huram, king of Tyre, answered in a letter sent to Solomon: 'Because the Lord loves His people, He has made you king over them.' Then Huram continued, 'Blessed be the Lord, the God of Israel, who has made heaven and earth, who has given King David a wise son, endowed with discretion and understanding, who will build a house for the Lord and a royal palace for himself. Now I am sending Huram-abi, a skilled man, endowed with understanding'" (2Ch. 2:11-12).

The King Faced About and Blessed Them All

"Then the king faced about and blessed all the assembly of Israel, while all the assembly of Israel was standing. He said, 'Blessed be the Lord, the God of Israel, who spoke with His mouth to my father David and has fulfilled it with His hands, saying, "Since the day that I brought My people from the land of Egypt, I did not choose a city out of all the tribes of Israel in which to build a house that My name might be there, nor did I choose any man for a leader over My people Israel; but I have chosen Jerusalem that My name might be there, and I have chosen David to be over My people Israel." Now it was in the heart of my father David to build a house for the name of the Lord, the God of Israel. But the Lord said to my father David, "Because it was in your heart to build a house for My name, you did well that it was in your heart. Nevertheless you shall not build the house, but your son who will be born to you, he shall build the house for My name." Now the Lord has fulfilled His word which He spoke; for I have risen in the place of my father David and sit on the throne of Israel, as the Lord promised, and have built the house for the name of the Lord, the God of Israel. There I have set the ark in which is the covenant of the Lord, which He made with the sons of Israel'" (2Ch. 6:3-11).

Chapter Two

Blessed Be the Lord Your God Who Delighted in You

"Now when the queen of Sheba heard of the fame of Solomon, she came to Jerusalem to test Solomon with difficult questions. She had a very large retinue, with camels carrying spices and a large amount of gold and precious stones; and when she came to Solomon, she spoke with him about all that was on her heart. Solomon answered all her questions; nothing was hidden from Solomon which he did not explain to her. When the queen of Sheba had seen the wisdom of Solomon, the house which he had built, the food at his table, the seating of his servants, the attendance of his ministers and their attire, his cupbearers and their attire, and his stairway by which he went up to the house of the Lord, she was breathless. Then she said to the king, 'It was a true report which I heard in my own land about your words and your wisdom. Nevertheless I did not believe their reports until I came and my eyes had seen it. And behold, the half of the greatness of your wisdom was not told me. You surpass the report that I heard. How blessed are your men, how blessed are these your servants who stand before you continually and hear your wisdom. Blessed be the Lord your God who delighted in you, setting you on His throne as king for the Lord your God; because your God loved Israel establishing them forever, therefore He made you king over them, to do justice and righteousness.' Then she gave the king one hundred and twenty talents of gold and a very great amount of spices and precious stones; there had never been spice like that which the queen of Sheba gave to King Solomon" (2Ch. 9:1-9).

They Blessed the Lord in the Valley of Beracah

"When Judah came to the lookout of the wilderness, they looked toward the multitude, and behold, they were corpses lying on the ground, and no one had escaped. When Jehoshaphat and his people came to take their spoil, they found much among them, including goods, garments and valuable things which they took for themselves, more than they could carry. And they were three days taking the spoil because there was so much. Then on the fourth day they assembled in the valley of Beracah, for there they blessed the Lord. Therefore they have named that place 'The Valley of Beracah' until today. Every man of Judah and Jerusalem returned with Jehoshaphat at their head, returning to Jerusalem with joy, for the Lord had made them to rejoice over their enemies. They came to Jerusalem with harps, lyres and trumpets to the house of the Lord. And the dread of God was on all the kingdoms of the lands when they heard that the Lord had fought against the enemies of Israel. So the kingdom of Jehoshaphat was at peace, for his God gave him rest on all sides" (2Ch. 20:24-30).

The Levitical Priests Arose and Blessed the People

"Then the whole assembly decided to celebrate the feast another seven days, so they celebrated the seven days with joy. For Hezekiah king of Judah had contributed to the assembly 1,000 bulls and 7,000 sheep, and the princes had contributed to the assembly 1,000 bulls and 10,000 sheep; and a large number of priests consecrated themselves. All the assembly of Judah rejoiced, with the priests and the Levites and all the assembly that came from Israel, both the sojourners who came from the land of Israel and those living in Judah. So there was great joy in Jerusalem, because there was nothing like this in Jerusalem since the days of Solomon the son of David, king of Israel. Then the Levitical priests arose and blessed the people; and their voice was heard and their prayer came to His holy dwelling place, to heaven" (2Ch. 30:23-27).

Hezekiah and the Rulers Blessed the Lord and His People

"And Hezekiah appointed the divisions of the priests and the Levites by their divisions, each according to his service, both the priests and the Levites, for burnt offerings and for peace offerings, to minister and to give thanks and to praise in the gates of the camp of the Lord. He also appointed the king's portion of his goods for the burnt offerings, namely, for the morning and evening burnt offerings, and the burnt offerings for the sabbaths and for the new moons and for the fixed festivals, as it is written in the law of the Lord. Also he commanded the people who lived in Jerusalem to give the portion due to the priests and the Levites, that they might devote themselves to the law of the Lord. As soon as the order spread, the sons of Israel provided in abundance the first fruits of grain, new wine, oil, honey and of all the produce of the field;

and they brought in abundantly the tithe of all. The sons of Israel and Judah who lived in the cities of Judah also brought in the tithe of oxen and sheep, and the tithe of sacred gifts which were consecrated to the Lord their God, and placed them in heaps. In the third month they began to make the heaps, and finished them by the seventh month. When Hezekiah and the rulers came and saw the heaps, they blessed the Lord and His people Israel. Then Hezekiah questioned the priests and the Levites concerning the heaps. Azariah the chief priest of the house of Zadok said to him, 'Since the contributions began to be brought into the house of the Lord, we have had enough to eat with plenty left over, for the Lord has blessed His people, and this great quantity is left over'" (2Ch. 31:2-10).

IN THE BOOK OF EZRA

Blessed Be the Lord, the God of Our Fathers

"Blessed be the Lord, the God of our fathers, who has put such a thing as this in the king's heart, to adorn the house of the Lord which is in Jerusalem, and has extended lovingkindness to me before the king and his counselors and before all the king's mighty princes. Thus I was strengthened according to the hand of the Lord my God upon me, and I gathered leading men from Israel to go up with me" (Ezr. 7:27-28).

Chapter Two

IN THE BOOK OF NEHEMIAH

Ezra Blessed the Lord the Great God

"And all the people gathered as one man at the square which was in front of the Water Gate, and they asked Ezra the scribe to bring the book of the law of Moses which the Lord had given to Israel. Then Ezra the priest brought the law before the assembly of men, women and all who could listen with understanding, on the first day of the seventh month. He read from it before the square which was in front of the Water Gate from early morning until midday, in the presence of men and women, those who could understand; and all the people were attentive to the book of the law. Ezra the scribe stood at a wooden podium which they had made for the purpose. And beside him stood Mattithiah, Shema, Anaiah, Uriah, Hilkiah, and Maaseiah on his right hand; and Pedaiah, Mishael, Malchijah, Hashum, Hashbaddanah, Zechariah and Meshullam on his left hand. Ezra opened the book in the sight of all the people for he was standing above all the people; and when he opened it, all the people stood up. Then Ezra blessed the Lord the great God. And all the people answered, 'Amen, Amen!' while lifting up their hands; then they bowed low and worshiped the Lord with their faces to the ground. Also Jeshua, Bani, Sherebiah, Jamin, Akkub, Shabbethai, Hodiah, Maaseiah, Kelita, Azariah, Jozabad, Hanan, Pelaiah, the Levites, explained the law to the people while the people remained in their place. They read from the book, from the law of God, translating to give the sense so that they understood the reading" (Ne. 8:1-8).

Blessed and Exalted Above All Blessing and Praise

"Then the Levites, Jeshua, Kadmiel, Bani, Hashabneiah, Sherebiah, Hodiah, Shebaniah and Pethahiah, said, 'Arise, bless the Lord your God forever and ever! O may Your glorious name be blessed and exalted above all blessing and praise! You alone are the Lord. You have made the heavens, the heaven of heavens with all their host, the earth and all that is on it, the seas and all that is in them. You give life to all of them and the heavenly host bows down before You. You are the Lord God, who chose Abram and brought him out from Ur of the Chaldees, and gave him the name Abraham. You found his heart faithful before You, and made a covenant with him to give him the land of the Canaanite, of the Hittite and the Amorite, of the Perizzite, the Jebusite and the Girgashite—to give it to his descendants. And You have fulfilled Your promise, for You are righteous'" (Ne. 9:5-8).

The People Blessed All the Men Who Volunteered

"Now the leaders of the people lived in Jerusalem, but the rest of the people cast lots to bring one out of ten to live in Jerusalem, the holy city, while nine-tenths remained in the other cities. And the people blessed all the men who volunteered to live in Jerusalem" (Ne. 11:1-2).

Chapter Two

IN THE BOOK OF JOB

You Have Blessed the Work of His Hands

"Now there was a day when the sons of God came to present themselves before the Lord, and Satan also came among them. The Lord said to Satan, 'From where do you come?' Then Satan answered the Lord and said, 'From roaming about on the earth and walking around on it.' The Lord said to Satan, 'Have you considered My servant Job? For there is no one like him on the earth, a blameless and upright man, fearing God and turning away from evil.' Then Satan answered the Lord, 'Does Job fear God for nothing? Have You not made a hedge about him and his house and all that he has, on every side? You have blessed the work of his hands, and his possessions have increased in the land. But put forth Your hand now and touch all that he has; he will surely curse You to Your face.' Then the Lord said to Satan, 'Behold, all that he has is in your power, only do not put forth your hand on him.' So Satan departed from the presence of the Lord" (Job 1:6-12).

Blessed Be the Name of the Lord

"Then Job arose and tore his robe and shaved his head, and he fell to the ground and worshiped. He said, 'Naked I came from my mother's womb, and naked I shall return there. The Lord gave and the Lord has taken away. Blessed be the name of the Lord'" (Job 1:20-21).

Chapter Two

The Lord Blessed the Latter Days of Job

"The Lord restored the fortunes of Job when he prayed for his friends, and the Lord increased all that Job had twofold. Then all his brothers and all his sisters and all who had known him before came to him, and they ate bread with him in his house; and they consoled him and comforted him for all the adversities that the Lord had brought on him. And each one gave him one piece of money, and each a ring of gold. The Lord blessed the latter days of Job more than his beginning; and he had 14,000 sheep and 6,000 camels and 1,000 yoke of oxen and 1,000 female donkeys. He had seven sons and three daughters. He named the first Jemimah, and the second Keziah, and the third Keren-happuch. In all the land no women were found so fair as Job's daughters; and their father gave them inheritance among their brothers. After this, Job lived 140 years, and saw his sons and his grandsons, four generations. And Job died, an old man and full of days" (Job 42:10-17).

IN THE BOOK OF PSALMS

Blessed Is the Man Who Does Not Walk in the Counsel of the Wicked

"How blessed is the man who does not walk in the counsel of the wicked, nor stand in the path of sinners, nor sit in the seat of scoffers! But his delight is in the law of the Lord, and in His law he meditates day and night. He will be like a tree firmly planted by streams of water, which yields its fruit in its season and its leaf does not wither; and in whatever he does, he prospers" (Ps. 1:1-3).

How Blessed Are All Who Take Refuge in Him

"Now therefore, O kings, show discernment; Take warning, O judges of the earth. Worship the Lord with reverence and rejoice with trembling. Do homage to the Son, that He not become angry, and you perish in the way, for His wrath may soon be kindled. How blessed are all who take refuge in Him" (Ps. 2:10-12)!

Blessed Be My Rock

"The Lord lives, and blessed be my rock; and exalted be the God of my salvation, the God who executes vengeance for me, and subdues peoples under me. He delivers me from my enemies; surely You lift me above those who rise up against me; You rescue me from the violent man. Therefore I will give thanks to You among the nations, O Lord, and I will sing praises to Your name. He gives great deliverance to His king, and shows lovingkindness to His anointed, to David and his descendants forever" (Ps. 18:46-50).

You Make Him Most Blessed Forever

"O LORD, in Your strength the king will be glad, and in Your salvation how greatly he will rejoice! You have given him his heart's desire, and You have not withheld the request of his lips. For You meet him with the blessings of good things; You set a crown of fine gold on his head. He asked life of You, You gave it to him, length of days forever and ever. His glory is great through Your salvation, splendor and majesty You place upon him. For You make him most blessed forever; You make him joyful with gladness in Your presence" (Ps. 21:1-6).

Blessed Be the Lord Who Heard the Voice of My Supplication

"Blessed be the Lord, because He has heard the voice of my supplication. The Lord is my strength and my shield; my heart trusts in Him, and I am helped; Therefore my heart exults, and with my song I shall thank Him. The Lord is their strength, and He is a saving defense to His anointed. Save Your people and bless Your inheritance; be their shepherd also, and carry them forever" (Ps. 28:6-9).

Blessed Be the Lord

"How great is Your goodness, which You have stored up for those who fear You, which You have wrought for those who take refuge in You, before the sons of men! You hide them in the secret place of Your presence from the conspiracies of man; You keep them secretly in a shelter from the strife of tongues. Blessed be the Lord, for He has made marvelous His lovingkindness to me in a besieged city. As for me, I said in my alarm, 'I am cut off from before Your eyes'; nevertheless You heard the voice of my supplications when I cried to You. O love the Lord, all you His godly ones! The Lord preserves the faithful and fully recompenses the proud doer. Be strong and let your heart take courage, all you who hope in the Lord" (Ps. 31:19-24).

How Blessed Is He Whose Transgression Is Forgiven

"How blessed is he whose transgression is forgiven, whose sin is covered! How blessed is the man to whom the Lord does not impute iniquity, and in whose spirit there is no deceit" (Ps. 32:1-2)!

How Blessed Is the Man to Whom the Lord Does Not Impute Iniquity

"How blessed is he whose transgression is forgiven, whose sin is covered! How blessed is the man to whom the Lord does not impute iniquity, and in whose spirit there is no deceit" (Ps. 32:1-2)!

Blessed Is the Nation Whose God Is the Lord

"By the word of the Lord the heavens were made, and by the breath of His mouth all their host. He gathers the waters of the sea together as a heap; He lays up the deeps in storehouses. Let all the earth fear the Lord; let all the inhabitants of the world stand in awe of Him. For He spoke, and it was done; He commanded, and it stood fast. The Lord nullifies the counsel of the nations; He frustrates the plans of the peoples. The counsel of the Lord stands forever, the plans of His heart from generation to generation. Blessed is the nation whose God is the Lord, the people whom He has chosen for His own inheritance" (Ps. 33:6-12).

Chapter Two

How Blessed Is the Man Who Takes Refuge in Him

"O taste and see that the Lord is good; how blessed is the man who takes refuge in Him! O fear the Lord, you His saints; for to those who fear Him there is no want. The young lions do lack and suffer hunger; but they who seek the Lord shall not be in want of any good thing. Come, you children, listen to me; I will teach you the fear of the Lord. Who is the man who desires life and loves length of days that he may see good? Keep your tongue from evil And your lips from speaking deceit. Depart from evil and do good; seek peace and pursue it" (Ps. 34:8-14).

For Those Blessed by Him Will Inherit the Land

"Better is the little of the righteous than the abundance of many wicked. For the arms of the wicked will be broken, but the Lord sustains the righteous. The Lord knows the days of the blameless, and their inheritance will be forever. They will not be ashamed in the time of evil, and in the days of famine they will have abundance. But the wicked will perish; and the enemies of the Lord will be like the glory of the pastures, they vanish—like smoke they vanish away. The wicked borrows and does not pay back, but the righteous is gracious and gives. For those blessed by Him will inherit the land, but those cursed by Him will be cut off" (Ps. 37:16-22).

Blessed Is the Man Who Makes the Lord His Trust

"How blessed is the man who has made the Lord his trust, And has not turned to the proud, nor to those who lapse into falsehood. Many, O Lord my God, are the wonders which You have done, and Your thoughts toward us; there is none to compare with You. If I would declare and speak of them, they would be too numerous to count" (Ps. 40:4-5).

How Blessed Is He Who Considers the Helpless

"How blessed is he who considers the helpless; The Lord will deliver him in a day of trouble. The Lord will protect him and keep him alive, and he shall be called blessed upon the earth; and do not give him over to the desire of his enemies. The Lord will sustain him upon his sickbed; In his illness, You restore him to health" (Ps. 41:1-3).

Blessed Be the Lord, the God of Israel

"But You, O Lord, be gracious to me and raise me up, That I may repay them. By this I know that You are pleased with me, because my enemy does not shout in triumph over me. As for me, You uphold me in my integrity, and You set me in Your presence forever. Blessed be the Lord, the God of Israel, From everlasting to everlasting. Amen and Amen" (Ps. 41:10-13).

Chapter Two

God Has Blessed You Forever

"My heart overflows with a good theme; I address my verses to the King; my tongue is the pen of a ready writer. You are fairer than the sons of men; grace is poured upon Your lips; therefore God has blessed You forever" (Ps. 45:1-2).

How Blessed Is the One Whom You Choose and Bring Near to You

"There will be silence before You, and praise in Zion, O God, and to You the vow will be performed. O You who hear prayer, to You all men come. Iniquities prevail against me; as for our transgressions, You forgive them. How blessed is the one whom You choose and bring near to You to dwell in Your courts. We will be satisfied with the goodness of Your house, Your holy temple" (Ps. 65:1-4).

Blessed Be God, Who Has Not Turned Away My Prayer

"Come and hear, all who fear God, and I will tell of what He has done for my soul. I cried to Him with my mouth, and He was extolled with my tongue. If I regard wickedness in my heart, the Lord will not hear; but certainly God has heard; He has given heed to the voice of my prayer. Blessed be God, who has not turned away my prayer nor His lovingkindness from me" (Ps. 66:16-20).

Chapter Two

Blessed be the Lord, Who Daily Bears Our Burden

"Blessed be the Lord, who daily bears our burden, the God who is our salvation. God is to us a God of deliverances; and to God the Lord belong escapes from death. Surely God will shatter the head of His enemies, the hairy crown of him who goes on in his guilty deeds. The Lord said, 'I will bring them back from Bashan. I will bring them back from the depths of the sea; that your foot may shatter them in blood, the tongue of your dogs may have its portion from your enemies'" (Ps. 68:19-23).

Blessed Be God

"Sing to God, O kingdoms of the earth, sing praises to the Lord, to Him who rides upon the highest heavens, which are from ancient times; behold, He speaks forth with His voice, a mighty voice. Ascribe strength to God; His majesty is over Israel And His strength is in the skies. O God, You are awesome from Your sanctuary. The God of Israel Himself gives strength and power to the people. Blessed be God" (Ps. 68:32-35)!

Let All Nations Call Him Blessed

"May there be abundance of grain in the earth on top of the mountains; its fruit will wave like the cedars of Lebanon; and may those from the city flourish like vegetation of the earth. May his name endure forever; may his name increase as long as the sun shines; and let men bless themselves by him; let all nations call him blessed" (Ps. 72:16-17).

Blessed Be the Lord Who Alone Works Wonders

"Blessed be the Lord God, the God of Israel, who alone works wonders. And blessed be His glorious name forever; and may the whole earth be filled with His glory. Amen, and Amen" (Ps. 72:18-19).

Blessed Are Those Who Dwell in Your House

"How lovely are Your dwelling places, O Lord of hosts! My soul longed and even yearned for the courts of the Lord; my heart and my flesh sing for joy to the living God. The bird also has found a house, and the swallow a nest for herself, where she may lay her young, Even Your altars, O Lord of hosts, my King and my God. How blessed are those who dwell in Your house! They are ever praising You" (Ps. 84:1-4).

Blessed Is the Man Whose Strength Is in You

"How blessed is the man whose strength is in You, In whose heart are the highways to Zion! Passing through the valley of Baca they make it a spring; The early rain also covers it with blessings. They go from strength to strength, Every one of them appears before God in Zion" (Ps. 84:5-7).

How Blessed Is the Man Who Trusts in You

"O Lord God of hosts, hear my prayer; Give ear, O God of Jacob! Behold our shield, O God, and look upon the face of Your anointed. For a day in

Your courts is better than a thousand outside. I would rather stand at the threshold of the house of my God than dwell in the tents of wickedness. For the Lord God is a sun and shield; the Lord gives grace and glory; no good thing does He withhold from those who walk uprightly. O Lord of hosts, How blessed is the man who trusts in You" (Ps. 84:8-12)!

How Blessed Are the People Who Know the Joyful Sound

"The heavens are Yours, the earth also is Yours; the world and all it contains, You have founded them. The north and the south, You have created them; Tabor and Hermon shout for joy at Your name. You have a strong arm; Your hand is mighty, Your right hand is exalted. Righteousness and justice are the foundation of Your throne; lovingkindness and truth go before You. How blessed are the people who know the joyful sound! O Lord, they walk in the light of Your countenance. In Your name they rejoice all the day, and by Your righteousness they are exalted. For You are the glory of their strength, and by Your favor our horn is exalted. For our shield belongs to the Lord, and our king to the Holy One of Israel. Once You spoke in vision to Your godly ones, and said, 'I have given help to one who is mighty; I have exalted one chosen from the people'" (Ps. 89:11-19).

Chapter Two

Blessed Is the Man Whom You Chasten

"Blessed is the man whom You chasten, O Lord, and whom You teach out of Your law; that You may grant him relief from the days of adversity, until a pit is dug for the wicked. For the Lord will not abandon His people, nor will He forsake His inheritance. For judgment will again be righteous, and all the upright in heart will follow it. Who will stand up for me against evildoers? Who will take his stand for me against those who do wickedness" (Ps. 94:12-16)?

How Blessed Are Those Who Keep Justice

"Praise the Lord! Oh give thanks to the Lord, for He is good; For His lovingkindness is everlasting. Who can speak of the mighty deeds of the Lord, or can show forth all His praise? How blessed are those who keep justice, who practice righteousness at all times" (Ps. 106:1-3)!

Blessed the Lord from Everlasting to Everlasting

"Nevertheless He looked upon their distress When He heard their cry; and He remembered His covenant for their sake, and relented according to the greatness of His lovingkindness. He also made them objects of compassion in the presence of all their captors. Save us, O Lord our God, and gather us from among the nations, to give thanks to Your holy name and glory in Your praise. Blessed be the Lord, the God of Israel, from everlasting even to everlasting. And let all the people say, 'Amen.' Praise the Lord" (Ps. 106:44-48)!

How Blessed Is the Man Who Fears the Lord

"Praise the Lord! How blessed is the man who fears the Lord, who greatly delights in His commandments. His descendants will be mighty on earth; the generation of the upright will be blessed. Wealth and riches are in his house, and his righteousness endures forever. Light arises in the darkness for the upright; He is gracious and compassionate and righteous. It is well with the man who is gracious and lends; He will maintain his cause in judgment. For he will never be shaken; the righteous will be remembered forever" (Ps. 112:1-6).

Blessed Be the Name of the Lord

"Praise the Lord! Praise, O servants of the Lord, Praise the name of the Lord. Blessed be the name of the Lord from this time forth and forever. From the rising of the sun to its setting the name of the Lord is to be praised. The Lord is high above all nations; His glory is above the heavens" (Ps. 113:1-4).

Blessed of the Lord, Maker of Heaven and Earth

"O Israel, trust in the Lord; He is their help and their shield. O house of Aaron, trust in the Lord; He is their help and their shield. You who fear the Lord, trust in the Lord; He is their help and their shield. The Lord has been mindful of us; He will bless us; He will bless the house of Israel; He will bless the house of Aaron. He will bless those who fear the Lord, the small together with the great. May the Lord give you increase, You and your children. May you be blessed of the Lord, maker of heaven and earth" (Ps. 115:9-15).

Blessed Is He Who Comes in the Name of the Lord

"The stone which the builders rejected has become the chief corner stone. This is the Lord's doing; it is marvelous in our eyes. This is the day which the Lord has made; let us rejoice and be glad in it. O Lord, do save, we beseech You; O Lord, we beseech You, do send prosperity! Blessed is the one who comes in the name of the Lord; we have blessed you from the house of the Lord. The Lord is God, and He has given us light; bind the festival sacrifice with cords to the horns of the altar. You are my God, and I give thanks to You; You are my God, I extol You. Give thanks to the Lord, for He is good; for His lovingkindness is everlasting" (Ps. 118:22-29).

How Blessed Are Those Whose Way Is Blameless

"How blessed are those whose way is blameless, who walk in the law of the Lord. How blessed are those who observe His testimonies, who seek Him with all their heart. They also do no unrighteousness; they walk in His ways. You have ordained Your precepts, that we should keep them diligently. Oh that my ways may be established to keep Your statutes! Then I shall not be ashamed when I look upon all Your commandments. I shall give thanks to You with uprightness of heart, when I learn Your righteous judgments. I shall keep Your statutes; do not forsake me utterly" (Ps. 119:1-8)!

Blessed Are You, O Lord; Teach Me Your Statutes

"How can a young man keep his way pure? By keeping it according to Your word. With all my heart I have sought You; do not let me wander from Your commandments. Your word I have treasured in my heart, that I may not sin against You. Blessed are You, O Lord; teach me Your statutes. With my lips I have told of all the ordinances of Your mouth. I have rejoiced in the way of Your testimonies, as much as in all riches. I will meditate on Your precepts and regard Your ways. I shall delight in Your statutes; I shall not forget Your word" (Ps. 119:9-16).

Blessed Be the Lord, Who Has Not Given Us to Be Torn by Their Teeth

"Blessed be the Lord, who has not given us to be torn by their teeth. Our soul has escaped as a bird out of the snare of the trapper; the snare is broken and we have escaped. Our help is in the name of the Lord, who made heaven and earth" (Ps. 124:6-8).

How Blessed Is the Man Whose Quiver Is Full

"Behold, children are a gift of the Lord, the fruit of the womb is a reward. Like arrows in the hand of a warrior, so are the children of one's youth. How blessed is the man whose quiver is full of them;

they will not be ashamed when they speak with their enemies in the gate" (Ps. 127:3-5).

How Blessed Is Everyone Who Fears the Lord

"How blessed is everyone who fears the Lord, who walks in His ways. When you shall eat of the fruit of your hands, you will be happy and it will be well with you. Your wife shall be like a fruitful vine within your house, Your children like olive plants around your table. Behold, for thus shall the man be blessed who fears the Lord" (Ps. 128:1-4).

Blessed Be the Lord from Zion

"O house of Israel, bless the Lord; O house of Aaron, bless the Lord; O house of Levi, bless the Lord; you who revere the Lord, bless the Lord. Blessed be the Lord from Zion, who dwells in Jerusalem. Praise the Lord" (Ps. 135:19-21)!

How Blessed Will Be the One Who Repays You

"Remember, O Lord, against the sons of Edom The day of Jerusalem, Who said, 'Raze it, raze it To its very foundation.' O daughter of Babylon, you devastated one, how blessed will be the one who repays you with the recompense with which you have repaid us. How blessed will be the one who seizes and dashes your little ones against the rock" (Ps. 137:7-9).

Chapter Two

Blessed Be the Lord, My Rock

"Blessed be the Lord, my rock, who trains my hands for war, and my fingers for battle; my lovingkindness and my fortress, my stronghold and my deliverer, my shield and He in whom I take refuge, who subdues my people under me. O Lord, what is man, that You take knowledge of him? Or the son of man, that You think of him? Man is like a mere breath; his days are like a passing shadow. Bow Your heavens, O Lord, and come down; touch the mountains, that they may smoke. Flash forth lightning and scatter them; send out Your arrows and confuse them. Stretch forth Your hand from on high; rescue me and deliver me out of great waters, out of the hand of aliens whose mouths speak deceit, and whose right hand is a right hand of falsehood" (Ps. 144:1-8).

How Blessed Are the People Who Are so Situated

"Let our sons in their youth be as grown-up plants, and our daughters as corner pillars fashioned as for a palace; let our garners be full, furnishing every kind of produce, and our flocks bring forth thousands and ten thousands in our fields; let our cattle bear without mishap and without loss, let there be no outcry in our streets! How blessed are the people who are so situated; how blessed are the people whose God is the Lord" (Ps. 144:12-15)!

Chapter Two

How Blessed Is He Whose Help Is the God of Jacob

"Praise the Lord! Praise the Lord, O my soul! I will praise the Lord while I live; I will sing praises to my God while I have my being. Do not trust in princes, in mortal man, in whom there is no salvation. His spirit departs, he returns to the earth; in that very day his thoughts perish. How blessed is he whose help is the God of Jacob, whose hope is in the Lord his God, who made heaven and earth, the sea and all that is in them; Who keeps faith forever; who executes justice for the oppressed; who gives food to the hungry. The Lord sets the prisoners free" (Ps. 146:1-7).

He Has Blessed Your Sons Within You

"Praise the Lord, O Jerusalem! Praise your God, O Zion! For He has strengthened the bars of your gates; He has blessed your sons within you. He makes peace in your borders; He satisfies you with the finest of the wheat. He sends forth His command to the earth; His word runs very swiftly. He gives snow like wool; He scatters the frost like ashes. He casts forth His ice as fragments; who can stand before His cold? He sends forth His word and melts them; He causes His wind to blow and the waters to flow. He declares His words to Jacob, His statutes and His ordinances to Israel. He has not dealt thus with any nation; and as for His ordinances, they have not known them. Praise the Lord" (Ps. 147:12-20)!

Chapter Two

IN THE BOOK OF PROVERBS

How Blessed Is the Man Who Finds Wisdom

"How blessed is the man who finds wisdom and the man who gains understanding. For her profit is better than the profit of silver and her gain better than fine gold. She is more precious than jewels; and nothing you desire compares with her. Long life is in her right hand; in her left hand are riches and honor. Her ways are pleasant ways and all her paths are peace. She is a tree of life to those who take hold of her, and happy are all who hold her fast" (Pr. 3:13-18).

Let Your Fountain Be Blessed

"Drink water from your own cistern and fresh water from your own well. Should your springs be dispersed abroad, streams of water in the streets? Let them be yours alone and not for strangers with you. Let your fountain be blessed, and rejoice in the wife of your youth. As a loving hind and a graceful doe, let her breasts satisfy you at all times; be exhilarated always with her love. For why should you, my son, be exhilarated with an adulteress and embrace the bosom of a foreigner? For the ways of a man are before the eyes of the Lord, and He watches all his paths. His own iniquities will capture the wicked, and he will be held with the cords of his sin. He will die for lack of instruction, and in the greatness of his folly he will go astray" (Pr. 5:15-23).

For Blessed Are They Who Keep My Ways

"Now therefore, O sons, listen to me, for blessed are they who keep my ways. Heed instruction and be wise, and do not neglect it. Blessed is the man who listens to me, watching daily at my gates, waiting at my doorposts. For he who finds me finds life and obtains favor from the Lord. But he who sins against me injures himself; all those who hate me love death" (Pr. 8:32-36).

The Righteous Is Blessed

"The memory of the righteous is blessed, but the name of the wicked will rot" (Pr. 10:7).

Blessed Is He Who Trusts in the Lord

"He who gives attention to the word will find good, and blessed is he who trusts in the Lord" (Pr. 16:20).

Blessed Are His Sons After Him

"A righteous man who walks in his integrity—how blessed are his sons after him" (Pr. 20:7).

Will Not Be Blessed in the End

"An inheritance gained hurriedly at the beginning will not be blessed in the end" (Pr. 20:21).

Chapter Two

He Who Is Generous Will Be Blessed

"He who is generous will be blessed, for he gives some of his food to the poor" (Pr. 22:9).

How Blessed Is the Man Who Fears Always

"How blessed is the man who fears always, but he who hardens his heart will fall into calamity" (Pr. 28:14).

IN THE BOOK OF ECCLESIASTES

Blessed Are You, O Land, Whose King Is of Nobility

"He who digs a pit may fall into it, and a serpent may bite him who breaks through a wall. He who quarries stones may be hurt by them, and he who splits logs may be endangered by them. If the axe is dull and he does not sharpen its edge, then he must exert more strength. Wisdom has the advantage of giving success. If the serpent bites before being charmed, there is no profit for the charmer. Words from the mouth of a wise man are gracious, while the lips of a fool consume him; the beginning of his talking is folly and the end of it is wicked madness. Yet the fool multiplies words. No man knows what will happen, and who can tell him what will come after him? The toil of a fool so wearies him that he does not even know how to go to a city. Woe to you, O land, whose king is a lad and whose princes feast in the morning. Blessed are you, O land, whose king is of nobility and whose princes eat at the appropriate time — for strength and not for drunkenness. Through indolence the rafters sag, and through slackness the house leaks. Men prepare a meal for enjoyment, and wine makes life merry, and money is the answer to everything. Furthermore, in your bedchamber do not curse a king, and in your sleeping rooms do not curse a rich man, for a bird of the heavens will carry the sound and the winged creature will make the matter known" (Ecc. 10:8-20).

IN THE BOOK OF SONG OF SOLOMON

The Maidens Saw Her and Called Her Blessed

"You are as beautiful as Tirzah, my darling, as lovely as Jerusalem, as awesome as an army with banners. Turn your eyes away from me, for they have confused me; your hair is like a flock of goats that have descended from Gilead. Your teeth are like a flock of ewes which have come up from their washing, all of which bear twins, and not one among them has lost her young. Your temples are like a slice of a pomegranate behind your veil. There are sixty queens and eighty concubines, and maidens without number; but my dove, my perfect one, is unique: she is her mother's only daughter; she is the pure child of the one who bore her. The maidens saw her and called her blessed, the queens and the concubines also, and they praised her, saying, 'Who is this that grows like the dawn, as beautiful as the full moon, as pure as the sun, as awesome as an army with banners?' I went down to the orchard of nut trees to see the blossoms of the valley, to see whether the vine had budded or the pomegranates had bloomed. Before I was aware, my soul set me over the chariots of my noble people" (SS. 6:4-12).

IN THE BOOK OF ISAIAH

The Lord of Hosts Has Blessed

"In that day Israel will be the third party with Egypt and Assyria, a blessing in the midst of the earth, whom the Lord of hosts has blessed, saying, 'Blessed is Egypt My people, and Assyria the work of My hands, and Israel My inheritance'" (Is. 19:24-25).

How Blessed Are All Those Who Long for Him

"Therefore the Lord longs to be gracious to you, and therefore He waits on high to have compassion on you. For the Lord is a God of justice; how blessed are all those who long for Him" (Is. 30:18).

How Blessed Will You Be Who Sow Beside All Waters

"Rise up, you women who are at ease, and hear my voice; give ear to my word, you complacent daughters. Within a year and a few days you will be troubled, O complacent daughters; for the vintage is ended, and the fruit gathering will not come. Tremble, you women who are at ease; be troubled, you complacent daughters; strip, undress and put sackcloth on your waist, beat your breasts for the pleasant fields, for the fruitful vine, for the land of my people in which thorns and briars shall come up; yea, for all the joyful houses and for the jubilant city. Because the palace has been abandoned, the populated city forsaken. Hill and watch-tower have become caves forever, a delight for wild donkeys, a pasture for flocks; until the Spirit is poured out upon us from on high, and the wilderness becomes a fertile field, and the fertile field is considered as a forest. Then justice will dwell in the wilderness and righteousness will abide in the fertile field. And the work of righteousness will be peace, and the service of righteousness, quietness and confidence forever. Then my people will live in a peaceful habitation, and in secure dwellings and in undisturbed resting places; and it will hail when the forest comes down, and the city will be utterly laid low. How blessed will you be, you who sow beside all waters, who let out freely the ox and the donkey" (Is. 32:9-20).

I Blessed Him and Multiplied Him

"'Listen to me, you who pursue righteousness, who seek the Lord: look to the rock from which you were hewn and to the quarry from which you were dug. Look to Abraham your father and to Sarah who gave birth to you in pain; when he was but one I called him, then I blessed him and multiplied him.' Indeed, the Lord will comfort Zion; He will comfort all her waste places. And her wilderness He will make like Eden, and her desert like the garden of the Lord; joy and gladness will be found in her, thanksgiving and sound of a melody" (Is. 51:1-3).

Chapter Two

How Blessed Is the Man Who Does This

"Thus says the Lord, 'Preserve justice and do righteousness, for My salvation is about to come and My righteousness to be revealed. How blessed is the man who does this, and the son of man who takes hold of it; who keeps from profaning the sabbath, and keeps his hand from doing any evil.' Let not the foreigner who has joined himself to the Lord say, 'The Lord will surely separate me from His people.' Nor let the eunuch say, 'Behold, I am a dry tree.' For thus says the Lord, 'To the eunuchs who keep My sabbaths, and choose what pleases Me, and hold fast My covenant, to them I will give in My house and within My walls a memorial, and a name better than that of sons and daughters; I will give them an everlasting name which will not be cut off'" (Is. 56:1-5).

The Offspring Whom the Lord Has Blessed

"Then they will rebuild the ancient ruins, they will raise up the former devastations; and they will repair the ruined cities, the desolations of many generations. Strangers will stand and pasture your flocks, and foreigners will be your farmers and your vinedressers. But you will be called the priests of the Lord; you will be spoken of as ministers of our God. You will eat the wealth of nations, and in their riches you will boast. Instead of your shame you will have a double portion, and instead of humiliation they will shout for joy over their portion. Therefore they will possess a double portion in their land, everlasting joy will be theirs. For I, the Lord, love justice, I hate robbery in the burnt offering; and I will faithfully give them their recompense and make an everlasting covenant with them. Then their offspring will be known among the nations, and their descendants in the midst of the peoples. All who see them will recognize them because they are the offspring whom the Lord has blessed" (Is. 61:4-9).

Will Be Blessed by the God of Truth

"Therefore, thus says the Lord God, 'Behold, My servants will eat, but you will be hungry. Behold, My servants will drink, but you will be thirsty. Behold, My servants will rejoice, but you will be put to shame. Behold, My servants will shout joyfully with a glad heart, but you will cry out with a heavy heart, and you will wail with a broken spirit. You will leave your name for a curse to My chosen ones, and the Lord God will slay you. But My servants will be called by another name. Because he who is blessed in the earth will be blessed by the God of truth; and he who swears in the earth will swear by the God of truth; because the former troubles are forgotten, and because they are hidden from My sight'" (Is. 65:13-16)!

The Offspring of Those Blessed by the Lord

"For behold, I create new heavens and a new earth; and the former things will not be remembered or come to mind. But be glad and rejoice forever in what I create; for behold, I create Jerusalem for rejoicing and her people for gladness. I will also rejoice in Jerusalem and be glad in My people; and there will no longer be heard in her the voice of weeping and the sound of crying. No longer will there be in it an infant who lives but a few days, or an old man who does not live out his days; for the youth will die at the age of one hundred and the one who does not reach the age of one hundred will be thought accursed. They will build houses and inhabit them; they will also plant vineyards and eat their fruit. They will not build and another inhabit, they will not plant and another eat; for as the lifetime of a tree, so will be the days of My people, and My chosen ones will wear out the work of their hands. They will not labor in vain, or bear children for calamity; for they are the offspring of those blessed by the Lord, and their descendants with them. It will also come to pass that before they call, I will answer; and while they are still speaking, I will hear. The wolf and the lamb will graze together, and the lion will eat straw like the ox; and dust will be the serpent's food. They will do no evil or harm in all My holy mountain,' says the Lord" (Is. 65:17-25).

IN THE BOOK OF JEREMIAH

Blessed Is the Man Who Trusts in the Lord

"Thus says the Lord, 'Cursed is the man who trusts in mankind and makes flesh his strength, and whose heart turns away from the Lord. For he will be like a bush in the desert and will not see when prosperity comes, but will live in stony wastes in the wilderness, a land of salt without inhabitant. Blessed is the man who trusts in the Lord and whose trust is the Lord. For he will be like a tree planted by the water, that extends its roots by a stream and will not fear when the heat comes; but its leaves will be green, and it will not be anxious in a year of drought nor cease to yield fruit'" (Jer. 17:5-8).

IN THE BOOK OF EZEKIEL

Blessed Be the Glory of the Lord in His Place

"Then the Spirit lifted me up, and I heard a great rumbling sound behind me, 'Blessed be the glory of the Lord in His place.' And I heard the sound of the wings of the living beings touching one another and the sound of the wheels beside them, even a great rumbling sound. So the Spirit lifted me up and took me away; and I went embittered in the rage of my spirit, and the hand of the Lord was strong on me. Then I came to the exiles who lived beside the river Chebar at Tel-abib, and I sat there seven days where they were living, causing consternation among them" (Eze. 3:12-15).

IN THE BOOK OF DANIEL

Daniel Blessed the God of Heaven

"Then Daniel went to his house and informed his friends, Hananiah, Mishael and Azariah, about the matter, so that they might request compassion from the God of heaven concerning this mystery, so that Daniel and his friends would not be destroyed with the rest of the wise men of Babylon. Then the mystery was revealed to Daniel in a night vision. Then Daniel blessed the God of heaven; Daniel said,

'Let the name of God be blessed forever and ever, for wisdom and power belong to Him. It is He who changes the times and the epochs; He removes kings and establishes kings; He gives wisdom to wise men and knowledge to men of understanding. It is He who reveals the profound and hidden things; He knows what is in the darkness, and the light dwells with Him. To You, O God of my fathers, I give thanks and praise, for You have given me wisdom and power; even now You have made known to me what we requested of You, for You have made known to us the king's matter'" (Da. 2:17-23).

Blessed Be the God of Shadrach, Meshach and Abed-nego

"Nebuchadnezzar responded and said, 'Blessed be the God of Shadrach, Meshach and Abed-nego, who has sent His angel and delivered His servants who put their trust in Him, violating the king's command, and yielded up their bodies so as not to serve or worship any god except their own God. Therefore I make a decree that any people, nation or tongue that speaks anything offensive against the God of Shadrach, Meshach and Abed-nego shall be torn limb from limb and their houses reduced to a rubbish heap, inasmuch as there is no other god who is able to deliver in this way.' Then the king caused Shadrach, Meshach and Abed-nego to prosper in the province of Babylon" (Da. 3:28-30).

Chapter Two

I Blessed the Most High

"But at the end of that period, I, Nebuchadnezzar, raised my eyes toward heaven and my reason returned to me, and I blessed the Most High and praised and honored Him who lives forever; for His dominion is an everlasting dominion, and His kingdom endures from generation to generation. All the inhabitants of the earth are accounted as nothing, but He does according to His will in the host of heaven and among the inhabitants of earth; and no one can ward off His hand Or say to Him, 'What have You done?' At that time my reason returned to me. And my majesty and splendor were restored to me for the glory of my kingdom, and my counselors and my nobles began seeking me out; so I was reestablished in my sovereignty, and surpassing greatness was added to me. Now I, Nebuchadnezzar, praise, exalt and honor the King of heaven, for all His works are true and His ways just, and He is able to humble those who walk in pride" (Da. 4:34-37).

How Blessed Is He Who Keeps Waiting

"Then I, Daniel, looked and behold, two others were standing, one on this bank of the river and the other on that bank of the river. And one said to the man dressed in linen, who was above the waters of the river, 'How long will it be until the end of these wonders?' I heard the man dressed in linen, who was above the waters of the river, as he raised his right hand and his left toward heaven, and swore by Him who lives forever that it would be for a time, times, and half a time; and as soon as they finish shattering the power of the holy people, all these events will be completed. As for me, I heard but could not understand; so I said, 'My lord, what will be the outcome of these events?' He said, 'Go your way, Daniel, for these words are concealed and sealed up until the end time. Many will be purged, purified and refined, but the wicked will act wickedly; and none of the wicked will understand, but those who have insight will understand. From the time that the regular sacrifice is abolished and the abomination of desolation is set up, there will be 1,290 days. How blessed is he who keeps waiting and attains to the 1,335 days! But as for you, go your way to the end; then you will enter into rest and rise again for your allotted portion at the end of the age'" (Da. 12:5-13).

IN THE BOOK OF ZECHARIAH

Blessed Be the Lord, For I Have Become Rich

"Thus says the Lord my God, 'Pasture the flock doomed to slaughter. Those who buy them slay them and go unpunished, and each of those who sell them says, "Blessed be the Lord, for I have become rich!" And their own shepherds have no pity on them. For I will no longer have pity on the inhabitants of the land,' declares the Lord; 'but behold, I will cause the men to fall, each into another's power and into the power of his king; and they will strike the land, and I will not deliver them from their power'" (Zec. 11:4-6).

Chapter Two

IN THE BOOK OF MALACHI

All the Nations Will Call You Blessed

'"Then I will rebuke the devourer for you, so that it will not destroy the fruits of the ground; nor will your vine in the field cast its grapes,' says the Lord of hosts. 'All the nations will call you blessed, for you shall be a delightful land,' says the Lord of hosts" (Mal. 3:11-12).

We Call the Arrogant Blessed

'"Your words have been arrogant against Me,' says the Lord. 'Yet you say, "What have we spoken against You?" You have said, "It is vain to serve God; and what profit is it that we have kept His charge, and that we have walked in mourning before the Lord of hosts? So now we call the arrogant blessed; not only are the doers of wickedness built up but they also test God and escape.'" Then those who feared the Lord spoke to one another, and the Lord gave attention and heard it, and a book of remembrance was written before Him for those who fear the Lord and who esteem His name. 'They will be Mine,' says the Lord of hosts, 'on the day that I prepare My own possession, and I will spare them as a man spares his own son who serves him'" (Mal. 3:13-17).

Chapter Three

BLESSED IN THE NEW TESTAMENT

IN THE BOOK OF MATTHEW

Blessed Are...

"Blessed are the poor in spirit, for theirs is the kingdom of heaven. Blessed are those who mourn, for they shall be comforted. Blessed are the gentle, for they shall inherit the earth. Blessed are those who hunger and thirst for righteousness, for they shall be satisfied. Blessed are the merciful, for they shall receive mercy. Blessed are the pure in heart, for they shall see God. Blessed are the peacemakers, for they shall be called sons of God. Blessed are those who have been persecuted for the sake of righteousness, for theirs is the kingdom of heaven. Blessed are you when people insult you and persecute you, and falsely say all kinds of evil against you because of Me" (Mt. 5:3-11).

Blessed Is He Who Does Not Take Offense

"When Jesus had finished giving instructions to His twelve disciples, He departed from there to teach and preach in their cities. Now when John, while imprisoned, heard of the works of Christ, he sent word by his disciples and said to Him, 'Are You the Expected One, or shall we look for someone else?' Jesus answered and said to them, 'Go and report to John what you hear and see: the BLIND RECEIVE SIGHT and the lame walk, the lepers are cleansed and the deaf hear, the dead are raised up, and the POOR HAVE THE GOSPEL PREACHED TO THEM. And blessed is he who does not take offense at Me'" (Mt. 11:1-6).

Blessed Are Your Eyes

"And the disciples came and said to Him, 'Why do You speak to them in parables?' Jesus answered them, 'To you it has been granted to know the mysteries of the kingdom of heaven, but to them it has not been granted. For whoever has, to him more shall be given, and he will have an abundance; but whoever does not have, even what he has shall be taken away from him. Therefore I speak to them in parables; because while seeing they do not see, and while hearing they do not hear, nor do they understand. In their case the prophecy of Isaiah is being fulfilled, which says, "YOU WILL KEEP ON HEARING, BUT WILL NOT UNDERSTAND; YOU WILL KEEP ON SEEING, BUT WILL NOT PERCEIVE; FOR THE HEART OF THIS PEOPLE HAS BECOME DULL, WITH THEIR EARS THEY SCARCELY HEAR, AND THEY HAVE CLOSED THEIR EYES, OTHERWISE THEY WOULD SEE WITH THEIR EYES, HEAR WITH THEIR EARS, AND UNDERSTAND WITH THEIR HEART AND RETURN, AND I WOULD HEAL THEM." But blessed are your eyes, because they see; and your ears, because they hear. For truly I say to you that many prophets and righteous men desired to see what you see, and did not see it, and to hear what you hear, and did not hear it'" (Mt. 13:10-17).

He Blessed the Food

"When it was evening, the disciples came to Him and said, 'This place is desolate and the hour is already late; so send the crowds away, that they may go into the villages and buy food for themselves.' But Jesus said to them, 'They do not need to go away; you give them something to eat!' They said to Him, 'We have here only five loaves and two fish.' And He said, 'Bring them here to Me.' Ordering the people to sit down on the grass, He took the five loaves and the two fish, and looking up toward heaven, He blessed the food, and breaking the loaves He gave them to the disciples, and the disciples gave them to the crowds, and they all ate and were satisfied. They picked up what was left over of the broken pieces, twelve full baskets. There were about five thousand men who ate, besides women and children" (Mt. 14:15-21).

Blessed Are You, Simon Barjona

"Now when Jesus came into the district of Caesarea Philippi, He was asking His disciples, 'Who do people say that the Son of Man is?' And they said, 'Some say John the Baptist; and others, Elijah; but still others, Jeremiah, or one of the prophets.' He said to them, 'But who do you say that I am?' Simon Peter answered, 'You are the Christ, the Son of the living God.' And Jesus said to him, 'Blessed are you, Simon Barjona, because flesh and blood did not reveal this to you, but My Father who is in heaven. I also say to you that you are Peter, and upon this rock I will build My church; and the gates of Hades will not overpower it. I will give you the keys of the kingdom of heaven; and whatever you bind on earth shall have been bound in heaven, and whatever you loose on earth shall have been loosed in heaven.' Then He warned the disciples that they should tell no one that He was the Christ" (Mt.

16:13-20).

Blessed Is He

"When they had approached Jerusalem and had come to Bethphage, at the Mount of Olives, then Jesus sent two disciples, saying to them, 'Go into the village opposite you, and immediately you will find a donkey tied there and a colt with her; untie them and bring them to Me. If anyone says anything to you, you shall say, "The Lord has need of them," and immediately he will send them.' This took place to fulfill what was spoken through the prophet: 'SAY TO THE DAUGHTER OF ZION, "BEHOLD YOUR KING IS COMING TO YOU, GENTLE, AND MOUNTED ON A DONKEY, EVEN ON A COLT, THE FOAL OF A BEAST OF BURDEN."' The disciples went and did just as Jesus had instructed them, and brought the donkey and the colt, and laid their coats on them; and He sat on the coats. Most of the crowd spread their coats in the road, and others were cutting branches from the trees and spreading them in the road. The crowds going ahead of Him, and those who followed, were shouting, 'Hosanna to the Son of David; BLESSED IS HE WHO COMES IN THE NAME OF THE LORD; Hosanna in the highest!' When He had entered Jerusalem, all the city was stirred, saying, 'Who is this?' And the crowds were saying, 'This is the prophet Jesus, from Nazareth in Galilee'" (Mt. 21:1-11).

Blessed Is He Who Comes in the Name of the Lord

"Therefore, behold, I am sending you prophets and wise men and scribes; some of them you will kill and crucify, and some of them you will scourge in your synagogues, and persecute from city to city, so that upon you may fall the guilt of all the righteous blood shed on earth, from the blood of righteous Abel to the blood of Zechariah, the son of Berechiah, whom you murdered between the temple and the altar. Truly I say to you, all these things will come upon this generation. Jerusalem, Jerusalem, who kills the prophets and stones those who are sent to her! How often I wanted to gather your children together, the way a hen gathers her chicks under her wings, and you were unwilling. Behold, your house is being left to you desolate! For I say to you, from now on you will not see Me until you say, 'BLESSED IS HE WHO COMES IN THE NAME OF THE LORD'" (Mt. 23:34-39)!

Blessed Is that Slave

"Who then is the faithful and sensible slave whom his master put in charge of his household to give them their food at the proper time? Blessed is that slave whom his master finds so doing when he comes. Truly I say to you that he will put him in charge of all his possessions. But if that evil slave says in his heart, 'My master is not coming for a long time,' and begins to beat his fellow slaves and eat and drink with drunkards; the master of that slave will come on a day when he does not expect him and at an hour which he does not know, and will cut him in pieces and assign him a place with the hypocrites; in that place there will be weeping and gnashing of teeth" (Mt. 24:45-51).

Chapter Three

Come, You Who Are Blessed of My Father

"Then the King will say to those on His right, 'Come, you who are blessed of My Father, inherit the kingdom prepared for you from the foundation of the world. For I was hungry, and you gave Me something to eat; I was thirsty, and you gave Me something to drink; I was a stranger, and you invited Me in; naked, and you clothed Me; I was sick, and you visited Me; I was in prison, and you came to Me.' Then the righteous will answer Him, 'Lord, when did we see You hungry, and feed You, or thirsty, and give You something to drink? And when did we see You a stranger, and invite You in, or naked, and clothe You? When did we see You sick, or in prison, and come to You?' The King will answer and say to them, 'Truly I say to you, to the extent that you did it to one of these brothers of Mine, even the least of them, you did it to Me'" (Mt. 25:34-40).

IN THE BOOK OF MARK

He Blessed the Food and Broke the Loaves

"The apostles gathered together with Jesus; and they reported to Him all that they had done and taught. And He said to them, 'Come away by yourselves to a secluded place and rest a while.' (For there were many people coming and going, and they did not even have time to eat.) They went away in the boat to a secluded place by themselves. The people saw them going, and many recognized them and ran there together on foot from all the cities, and got there ahead of them. When Jesus went ashore, He saw a large crowd, and He felt compassion for them because they were like sheep without a shepherd; and He began to teach them many things. When it was already quite late, His disciples came to Him and said, 'This place is desolate and it is already quite late; send them away so that they may go into the surrounding countryside and villages and buy themselves something to eat.' But He answered them, 'You give them something to eat!' And they said to Him, 'Shall we go and spend two hundred denarii on bread and give them something to eat?' And He said to them, 'How many loaves do you have? Go look!' And when they found out, they said, 'Five, and two fish.' And He commanded them all to sit down by groups on the green grass. They sat down in groups of hundreds and of fifties. And He took the five loaves and the two fish, and looking up toward heaven, He blessed the food and broke the loaves and He kept giving them to the disciples to set before them; and He divided up the two fish among them all. They all ate and were satisfied, and they picked up twelve full baskets of the broken pieces, and also of the fish. There were five thousand men who ate the loaves" (Mr. 6:30-44).

After He Had Blessed Them

"In those days, when there was again a large crowd and they had nothing to eat, Jesus called His disciples and said to them, 'I feel compassion for the people because they have remained with Me now three days and have nothing to eat. If I send them away hungry to their homes, they will faint on the way; and some of them have come from a great distance.' And His disciples answered Him, 'Where will anyone be able to find enough bread here in this desolate place to satisfy these people?' And He was asking them, 'How many loaves do you have?' And they said, 'Seven.' And He directed the people to sit down on the ground; and taking the seven loaves, He gave thanks and broke them, and started giving them to His disciples to serve to them, and they served them to the people. They also had a few small fish; and after He had blessed them, He ordered these to be served as well. And they ate and were satisfied; and they picked up seven large baskets full of what was left over of the broken pieces. About four thousand were there; and He sent them away. And immediately He entered the boat with His disciples and came to the district of Dalmanutha" (Mr. 8:1-10).

Blessed Is the Coming Kingdom

"As they approached Jerusalem, at Bethphage and Bethany, near the Mount of Olives, He sent two of His disciples, and said to them, 'Go into the village opposite you, and immediately as you enter it, you will find a colt tied there, on which no one yet has ever sat; untie it and bring it here. If anyone says to you, 'Why are you doing this?" you say, "The Lord has need of it"; and immediately he will send it back here.' They went away and found a colt tied at the door, outside in the street; and they untied it. Some of the bystanders were saying to them, 'What are you doing, untying the colt?' They spoke to them just as Jesus had told them, and they gave them permission. They brought the colt to Jesus and put their coats on it; and He sat on it. And many spread their coats in the road, and others spread leafy branches which they had cut from the fields. Those who went in front and those who followed were shouting: 'Hosanna! BLESSED IS HE WHO COMES IN THE NAME OF THE LORD; Blessed is the coming

kingdom of our father David; Hosanna in the highest'"
(Mr. 11:1-10)!

You the Christ, the Son of the Blessed One

"They led Jesus away to the high priest; and all
the chief priests and the elders and the scribes gathered
together. Peter had followed Him at a distance, right
into the courtyard of the high priest; and he was sitting
with the officers and warming himself at the fire. Now
the chief priests and the whole Council kept trying to
obtain testimony against Jesus to put Him to death, and
they were not finding any. For many were giving false
testimony against Him, but their testimony was not
consistent. Some stood up and began to give false
testimony against Him, saying, 'We heard Him say, "I
will destroy this temple made with hands, and in three
days I will build another made without hands."' Not
even in this respect was their testimony consistent. The
high priest stood up and came forward and questioned
Jesus, saying, 'Do You not answer? What is it that these
men are testifying against You?' But He kept silent and
did not answer. Again the high priest was questioning
Him, and saying to Him, 'Are You the Christ, the Son of
the Blessed One?' And Jesus said, 'I am; and you shall
see THE SON OF MAN SITTING AT THE RIGHT
HAND OF POWER, and COMING WITH THE
CLOUDS OF HEAVEN.' Tearing his clothes, the high
priest said, 'What further need do we have of witnesses?
You have heard the blasphemy; how does it seem to
you?' And they all condemned Him to be deserving of
death. Some began to spit at Him, and to blindfold Him,
and to beat Him with their fists, and to say to Him,
'Prophesy!' And the officers received Him with slaps in

the face" (Mr. 14:53-65).

IN THE BOOK OF LUKE

Blessed Is the Fruit of Your Womb

"Now at this time Mary arose and went in a hurry to the hill country, to a city of Judah, and entered the house of Zacharias and greeted Elizabeth. When Elizabeth heard Mary's greeting, the baby leaped in her womb; and Elizabeth was filled with the Holy Spirit. And she cried out with a loud voice and said, 'Blessed are you among women, and blessed is the fruit of your womb! And how has it happened to me, that the mother of my Lord would come to me? For behold, when the sound of your greeting reached my ears, the baby leaped in my womb for joy. And blessed is she who believed that there would be a fulfillment of what had been spoken to her by the Lord'" (Lk. 1:39-45).

All Generations Will Count Me Blessed

"And Mary said: 'My soul exalts the Lord, and my spirit has rejoiced in God my Savior. For He has had regard for the humble state of His bondslave; for behold, from this time on all generations will count me blessed. For the Mighty One has done great things for me; and holy is His name. AND HIS MERCY IS UPON GENERATION AFTER GENERATION TOWARD THOSE WHO FEAR HIM. He has done mighty deeds with His arm; He has scattered those who were proud in the thoughts of their heart. He has brought down rulers from their thrones, and has exalted those who were humble. HE HAS FILLED THE HUNGRY WITH GOOD

THINGS; and sent away the rich empty-handed. He has given help to Israel His servant, in remembrance of His mercy, as He spoke to our fathers, to Abraham and his descendants forever'" (Lk. 1:46-55).

Blessed Be the Lord God of Israel

"And his father Zacharias was filled with the Holy Spirit, and prophesied, saying: 'Blessed be the Lord God of Israel, For He has visited us and accomplished redemption for His people, and has raised up a horn of salvation for us in the house of David His servant—as He spoke by the mouth of His holy prophets from of old—salvation FROM OUR ENEMIES, and FROM THE HAND OF ALL WHO HATE US; to show mercy toward our fathers, and to remember His holy covenant, the oath which He swore to Abraham our father, to grant us that we, being rescued from the hand of our enemies, might serve Him without fear, in holiness and righteousness before Him all our days. And you, child, will be called the prophet of the Most High; for you will go on BEFORE THE LORD TO PREPARE HIS WAYS; to give to His people the knowledge of salvation by the forgiveness of their sins, because of the tender mercy of our God, with which the sunrise from on high will visit us, TO SHINE UPON THOSE WHO SIT IN DARKNESS AND THE SHADOW OF DEATH, to guide our feet into the way of peace'" (Lk. 1:67-79).

He Took Him into His Arms, and Blessed God

"And there was a man in Jerusalem whose name was Simeon; and this man was righteous and devout, looking for the consolation of Israel; and the Holy Spirit was upon him. And it had been revealed to him by the Holy Spirit that he would not see death before he had seen the Lord's Christ. And he came in the Spirit into the temple; and when the parents brought in the child Jesus, to carry out for Him the custom of the Law, then he took Him into his arms, and blessed God, and said, 'Now Lord, You are releasing Your bond-servant to depart in peace, According to Your word; for my eyes have seen Your salvation, which You have prepared in the presence of all peoples, A LIGHT OF REVELATION TO THE GENTILES, and the glory of Your people Israel'" (Lk. 2:25-32).

Blessed

"And turning His gaze toward His disciples, He began to say, 'Blessed are you who are poor, for yours is the kingdom of God. Blessed are you who hunger now, for you shall be satisfied. Blessed are you who weep now, for you shall laugh. Blessed are you when men hate you, and ostracize you, and insult you, and scorn your name as evil, for the sake of the Son of Man. Be glad in that day and leap for joy, for behold, your reward is great in heaven. For in the same way their fathers used to treat the prophets. But woe to you who are rich, for you are receiving your comfort in full. Woe to you who are well-fed now, for you shall be hungry. Woe to you who laugh now, for you shall mourn and weep. Woe to you when all men speak well of you, for their fathers used to treat the false prophets in the same way'" (Lk. 6:20-26).

Chapter Three

Blessed Is He Who Does Not Take Offense at Me

"The disciples of John reported to him about all these things. Summoning two of his disciples, John sent them to the Lord, saying, 'Are You the Expected One, or do we look for someone else?' When the men came to Him, they said, 'John the Baptist has sent us to You, to ask, 'Are You the Expected One, or do we look for someone else?' At that very time He cured many people of diseases and afflictions and evil spirits; and He gave sight to many who were blind. And He answered and said to them, 'Go and report to John what you have seen and heard: the BLIND RECEIVE SIGHT, the lame walk, the lepers are cleansed, and the deaf hear, the dead are raised up, the POOR HAVE THE GOSPEL PREACHED TO THEM. Blessed is he who does not take offense at Me'" (Lk. 7:18-23).

He Blessed Them, and Broke Them

"Now the day was ending, and the twelve came and said to Him, 'Send the crowd away, that they may go into the surrounding villages and countryside and find lodging and get something to eat; for here we are in a desolate place.' But He said to them, 'You give them something to eat!' And they said, 'We have no more than five loaves and two fish, unless perhaps we go and buy food for all these people.' (For there were about five thousand men.) And He said to His disciples, 'Have them sit down to eat in groups of about fifty each.' They did so, and had them all sit down. Then He took the five loaves and the two fish, and looking up to heaven, He blessed them, and broke them, and kept giving them to the disciples to set before the people. And they all ate and were satisfied; and the broken pieces which they had left over were picked up, twelve baskets full" (Lk. 9:12-17).

Blessed Are the Eyes Which See the Things You See

"Turning to the disciples, He said privately, 'Blessed are the eyes which see the things you see, for I say to you, that many prophets and kings wished to see the things which you see, and did not see them, and to hear the things which you hear, and did not hear them'" (Lk. 10:23-24).

Blessed Is the Womb that Bore You

"While Jesus was saying these things, one of the women in the crowd raised her voice and said to Him, 'Blessed is the womb that bore You and the breasts at which You nursed.' But He said, 'On the contrary, blessed are those who hear the word of God and observe it'" (Lk. 11:27-28).

Blessed Are Those Slaves

"Be dressed in readiness, and keep your lamps lit. Be like men who are waiting for their master when he returns from the wedding feast, so that they may immediately open the door to him when he comes and knocks. Blessed are those slaves whom the master will find on the alert when he comes; truly I say to you, that he will gird himself to serve, and have them recline at the table, and will come up and wait on them. Whether he comes in the second watch, or even in the third, and finds them so, blessed are those slaves" (Lk. 12:35-38).

Chapter Three

Blessed Is He

"Just at that time some Pharisees approached, saying to Him, 'Go away, leave here, for Herod wants to kill You.' And He said to them, 'Go and tell that fox, "Behold, I cast out demons and perform cures today and tomorrow, and the third day I reach My goal." Nevertheless I must journey on today and tomorrow and the next day; for it cannot be that a prophet would perish outside of Jerusalem. O Jerusalem, Jerusalem, the city that kills the prophets and stones those sent to her! How often I wanted to gather your children together, just as a hen gathers her brood under her wings, and you would not have it! Behold, your house is left to you desolate;and I say to you, you will not see Me until the time comes when you say, "BLESSED IS HE WHO COMES IN THE NAME OF THE LORD"'" (Lk. 13:31-35)!

You Will Be Blessed

"And He also went on to say to the one who had invited Him, 'When you give a luncheon or a dinner, do not invite your friends or your brothers or your relatives or rich neighbors, otherwise they may also invite you in return and that will be your repayment. But when you give a reception, invite the poor, the crippled, the lame, the blind, and you will be blessed, since they do not have the means to repay you; for you will be repaid at the resurrection of the righteous'" (Lk. 14:12-14).

Chapter Three

Blessed Is Everyone Who Will Eat Bread in the Kingdom of God

"When one of those who were reclining at the table with Him heard this, he said to Him, 'Blessed is everyone who will eat bread in the kingdom of God!' But He said to him, 'A man was giving a big dinner, and he invited many; and at the dinner hour he sent his slave to say to those who had been invited, "Come; for everything is ready now." But they all alike began to make excuses. The first one said to him, "I have bought a piece of land and I need to go out and look at it; please consider me excused." Another one said, "I have bought five yoke of oxen, and I am going to try them out; please consider me excused." Another one said, "I have married a wife, and for that reason I cannot come." And the slave came back and reported this to his master. Then the head of the household became angry and said to his slave, "Go out at once into the streets and lanes of the city and bring in here the poor and crippled and blind and lame." And the slave said, "Master, what you commanded has been done, and still there is room." And the master said to the slave, "Go out into the highways and along the hedges, and compel them to come in, so that my house may be filled. For I tell you, none of those men who were invited shall taste of my dinner"'" (Lk. 14:15-24).

Blessed Is the King

"When He approached Bethphage and Bethany, near the mount that is called Olivet, He sent two of the disciples, saying, 'Go into the village ahead of you; there, as you enter, you will find a colt tied on which no one yet has ever sat; untie it and bring it here. If anyone asks you, "Why are you untying it?" you shall say, "The Lord has need of it."' So those who were sent went away and found it just as He had told them. As they were untying the colt, its owners said to them, 'Why are you untying the colt?' They said, 'The Lord has need of it.' They brought it to Jesus, and they threw their coats on the colt and put Jesus on it. As He was going, they were spreading their coats on the road. As soon as He was approaching, near the descent of the Mount of Olives, the whole crowd of the disciples began to praise God joyfully with a loud voice for all the miracles which they had seen, shouting: 'BLESSED IS THE KING WHO COMES IN THE NAME OF THE LORD; Peace in heaven and glory in the highest!' Some of the Pharisees in the crowd said to Him, 'Teacher, rebuke Your disciples.' But Jesus answered, 'I tell you, if these become silent, the stones will cry out'" (Lk. 19:29-40)!

Blessed Are the Barren

"And following Him was a large crowd of the people, and of women who were mourning and lamenting Him. But Jesus turning to them said, 'Daughters of Jerusalem, stop weeping for Me, but weep for yourselves and for your children. For behold, the days are coming when they will say, "Blessed are the barren, and the wombs that never bore, and the breasts that never nursed." Then they will begin TO SAY TO THE MOUNTAINS, "FALL ON US," AND TO THE HILLS, "COVER US." For if they do these things when the tree is green, what will happen when it is dry'" (Lk. 23:27-31)?

Chapter Three

He Took the Bread and Blessed It

"And they approached the village where they were going, and He acted as though He were going farther. But they urged Him, saying, 'Stay with us, for it is getting toward evening, and the day is now nearly over.' So He went in to stay with them. When He had reclined at the table with them, He took the bread and blessed it, and breaking it, He began giving it to them. Then their eyes were opened and they recognized Him; and He vanished from their sight. They said to one another, 'Were not our hearts burning within us while He was speaking to us on the road, while He was explaining the Scriptures to us?' And they got up that very hour and returned to Jerusalem, and found gathered together the eleven and those who were with them, saying, 'The Lord has really risen and has appeared to Simon.' They began to relate their experiences on the road and how He was recognized by them in the breaking of the bread" (Lk. 24:28-35).

He Lifted up His Hands and Blessed Them

"And He led them out as far as Bethany, and He lifted up His hands and blessed them. While He was blessing them, He parted from them and was carried up into heaven. And they, after worshiping Him, returned to Jerusalem with great joy, and were continually in the temple praising God" (Lk. 24:50-53).

Chapter Three

IN THE BOOK OF JOHN

Blessed Is He Who Comes

"On the next day the large crowd who had come to the feast, when they heard that Jesus was coming to Jerusalem, took the branches of the palm trees and went out to meet Him, and began to shout, 'Hosanna! BLESSED IS HE WHO COMES IN THE NAME OF THE LORD, even the King of Israel.' Jesus, finding a young donkey, sat on it; as it is written, 'FEAR NOT, DAUGHTER OF ZION; BEHOLD, YOUR KING IS COMING, SEATED ON A DONKEY'S COLT.' These things His disciples did not understand at the first; but when Jesus was glorified, then they remembered that these things were written of Him, and that they had done these things to Him. So the people, who were with Him when He called Lazarus out of the tomb and raised him from the dead, continued to testify about Him. For this reason also the people went and met Him, because they heard that He had performed this sign. So the Pharisees said to one another, 'You see that you are not doing any good; look, the world has gone after Him'" (Jn. 12:12-19).

You Are Blessed if You Do Them

"So when He had washed their feet, and taken His garments and reclined at the table again, He said to them, 'Do you know what I have done to you? You call Me Teacher and Lord; and you are right, for so I am. If I then, the Lord and the Teacher, washed your feet, you also ought to wash one another's feet. For I gave you an example that you also should do as I did to you. Truly,

truly, I say to you, a slave is not greater than his master, nor is one who is sent greater than the one who sent him. If you know these things, you are blessed if you do them. I do not speak of all of you. I know the ones I have chosen; but it is that the Scripture may be fulfilled, "HE WHO EATS MY BREAD HAS LIFTED UP HIS HEEL AGAINST ME." From now on I am telling you before it comes to pass, so that when it does occur, you may believe that I am He. Truly, truly, I say to you, he who receives whomever I send receives Me; and he who receives Me receives Him who sent Me'" (Jn. 13:12-20).

Blessed Are They Who Did Not See, and Yet Believed

"But Thomas, one of the twelve, called Didymus, was not with them when Jesus came. So the other disciples were saying to him, 'We have seen the Lord!' But he said to them, 'Unless I see in His hands the imprint of the nails, and put my finger into the place of the nails, and put my hand into His side, I will not believe.' After eight days His disciples were again inside, and Thomas with them. Jesus came, the doors having been shut, and stood in their midst and said, 'Peace be with you.' Then He said to Thomas, 'Reach here with your finger, and see My hands; and reach here your hand and put it into My side; and do not be unbelieving, but believing.' Thomas answered and said to Him, 'My Lord and my God!' Jesus said to him, 'Because you have seen Me, have you believed? Blessed are they who did not see, and yet believed'" (Jn. 20:24-29).

IN THE BOOK OF ACTS

Shall Be Blessed

"And now, brethren, I know that you acted in ignorance, just as your rulers did also. But the things which God announced beforehand by the mouth of all the prophets, that His Christ would suffer, He has thus fulfilled. Therefore repent and return, so that your sins may be wiped away, in order that times of refreshing may come from the presence of the Lord; and that He may send Jesus, the Christ appointed for you, whom heaven must receive until the period of restoration of all things about which God spoke by the mouth of His holy prophets from ancient time. Moses said, 'THE LORD GOD WILL RAISE UP FOR YOU A PROPHET LIKE ME FROM YOUR BRETHREN; TO HIM YOU SHALL GIVE HEED to everything He says to you. And it will be that every soul that does not heed that prophet shall be utterly destroyed from among the people.' And likewise, all the prophets who have spoken, from Samuel and his successors onward, also announced these days. It is you who are the sons of the prophets and of the covenant which God made with your fathers, saying to Abraham, 'AND IN YOUR SEED ALL THE FAMILIES OF THE EARTH SHALL BE BLESSED.' For you first, God raised up His Servant and sent Him to bless you by turning every one of you from your wicked ways" (Ac. 3:17-26).

It Is More Blessed to Give than to Receive

"And now, behold, I know that all of you, among whom I went about preaching the kingdom, will no longer see my face. Therefore, I testify to you this day that I am innocent of the blood of all men. For I did not shrink from declaring to you the whole purpose of God. Be on guard for yourselves and for all the flock, among which the Holy Spirit has made you overseers, to shepherd the church of God which He purchased with His own blood. I know that after my departure savage wolves will come in among you, not sparing the flock; and from among your own selves men will arise, speaking perverse things, to draw away the disciples after them. Therefore be on the alert, remembering that night and day for a period of three years I did not cease to admonish each one with tears. And now I commend you to God and to the word of His grace, which is able to build you up and to give you the inheritance among all those who are sanctified. I have coveted no one's silver or gold or clothes. You yourselves know that these hands ministered to my own needs and to the men who were with me. In everything I showed you that by working hard in this manner you must help the weak and remember the words of the Lord Jesus, that He Himself said, 'It is more blessed to give than to receive'" (Ac. 20:25-35).

IN THE BOOK OF ROMANS

Who Is Blessed Forever

"Therefore God gave them over in the lusts of their hearts to impurity, so that their bodies would be dishonored among them. For they exchanged the truth of God for a lie, and worshiped and served the creature rather than the Creator, who is blessed forever. Amen" (Ro. 1:24-25).

Chapter Three

Blessed Are Those Who Have Been Forgiven

"What then shall we say that Abraham, our forefather according to the flesh, has found? For if Abraham was justified by works, he has something to boast about, but not before God. For what does the Scripture say? 'ABRAHAM BELIEVED GOD, AND IT WAS CREDITED TO HIM AS RIGHTEOUSNESS.' Now to the one who works, his wage is not credited as a favor, but as what is due. But to the one who does not work, but believes in Him who justifies the ungodly, his faith is credited as righteousness, just as David also speaks of the blessing on the man to whom God credits righteousness apart from works: 'BLESSED ARE THOSE WHOSE LAWLESS DEEDS HAVE BEEN FORGIVEN, AND WHOSE SINS HAVE BEEN COVERED. BLESSED IS THE MAN WHOSE SIN THE LORD WILL NOT TAKE INTO ACCOUNT'" (Ro. 4:1-8).

God Blessed Forever. Amen.

"I am telling the truth in Christ, I am not lying, my conscience testifies with me in the Holy Spirit, that I have great sorrow and unceasing grief in my heart. For I could wish that I myself were accursed, separated from Christ for the sake of my brethren, my kinsmen according to the flesh, who are Israelites, to whom belongs the adoption as sons, and the glory and the covenants and the giving of the Law and the temple service and the promises, whose are the fathers, and from whom is the Christ according to the flesh, who is over all, God blessed forever. Amen" (Ro. 9:1-5).

Chapter Three

IN THE BOOK OF 2 CORINTHIANS

Blessed Be the Father of Our Lord Jesus Christ

"Blessed be the God and Father of our Lord Jesus Christ, the Father of mercies and God of all comfort, who comforts us in all our affliction so that we will be able to comfort those who are in any affliction with the comfort with which we ourselves are comforted by God. For just as the sufferings of Christ are ours in abundance, so also our comfort is abundant through Christ. But if we are afflicted, it is for your comfort and salvation; or if we are comforted, it is for your comfort, which is effective in the patient enduring of the same sufferings which we also suffer; and our hope for you is firmly grounded, knowing that as you are sharers of our sufferings, so also you are sharers of our comfort" (2Co. 1:3-7).

He Who Is Blessed

"If I have to boast, I will boast of what pertains to my weakness. The God and Father of the Lord Jesus, He who is blessed forever, knows that I am not lying. In Damascus the ethnarch under Aretas the king was guarding the city of the Damascenes in order to seize me, and I was let down in a basket through a window in the wall, and so escaped his hands" (2Co. 11:30-33).

IN THE BOOK OF GALATIANS

All the Nations Will Be Blessed in You

"Even so Abraham BELIEVED GOD, AND IT WAS RECKONED TO HIM AS RIGHTEOUSNESS. Therefore, be sure that it is those who are of faith who are sons of Abraham. The Scripture, foreseeing that God would justify the Gentiles by faith, preached the gospel beforehand to Abraham, saying, 'ALL THE NATIONS WILL BE BLESSED IN YOU.' So then those who are of faith are blessed with Abraham, the believer" (Gal. 3:6-9).

IN THE BOOK OF EPHESIANS

Blessed Be the God

"Blessed be the God and Father of our Lord Jesus Christ, who has blessed us with every spiritual blessing in the heavenly places in Christ, just as He chose us in Him before the foundation of the world, that we would be holy and blameless before Him. In love He predestined us to adoption as sons through Jesus Christ to Himself, according to the kind intention of His will, to the praise of the glory of His grace, which He freely bestowed on us in the Beloved. In Him we have redemption through His blood, the forgiveness of our trespasses, according to the riches of His grace which He lavished on us. In all wisdom and insight He made known to us the mystery of His will, according to His kind intention which He purposed in Him with a view to an administration suitable to the fullness of the times, that is, the summing up of all things in Christ, things in the heavens and things on the earth. In Him also we have obtained an inheritance, having been predestined according to His purpose who works all things after the counsel of His will, to the end that we who were the first to hope in Christ would be to the praise of His glory. In Him, you also, after listening to the message of truth, the gospel of your salvation—having also believed, you were sealed in Him with the Holy Spirit of promise, who is given as a pledge of our inheritance, with a view to the redemption of God's own possession, to the praise of His glory" (Eph. 1:3-14).

IN THE BOOK OF 1 TIMOTHY

The Glorious Gospel of the Blessed God

"But we know that the Law is good, if one uses it lawfully, realizing the fact that law is not made for a righteous person, but for those who are lawless and rebellious, for the ungodly and sinners, for the unholy and profane, for those who kill their fathers or mothers, for murderers and immoral men and homosexuals and kidnappers and liars and perjurers, and whatever else is contrary to sound teaching, according to the glorious gospel of the blessed God, with which I have been entrusted" (1Ti. 1:8-11).

The Blessed King of Kings and Lord of Lords

"But flee from these things, you man of God, and pursue righteousness, godliness, faith, love, perseverance and gentleness. Fight the good fight of faith; take hold of the eternal life to which you were called, and you made the good confession in the presence of many witnesses. I charge you in the presence of God, who gives life to all things, and of Christ Jesus, who testified the good confession before Pontius Pilate, that you keep the commandment without stain or reproach until the appearing of our Lord Jesus Christ, which He will bring about at the proper time — He who is the blessed and only Sovereign, the King of kings and Lord of lords, who alone possesses immortality and dwells in unapproachable light, whom no man has seen or can see. To Him be honor and eternal dominion! Amen" (1Ti. 6:11-16).

IN THE BOOK OF TITUS

Looking for the Blessed Hope

"For the grace of God has appeared, bringing salvation to all men, instructing us to deny ungodliness and worldly desires and to live sensibly, righteously and godly in the present age, looking for the blessed hope and the appearing of the glory of our great God and Savior, Christ Jesus, who gave Himself for us to redeem us from every lawless deed, and to purify for Himself a people for His own possession, zealous for good deeds" (Tit. 2:11-14).

IN THE BOOK OF HEBREWS

He Was Returning from the Slaughter of the Kings and Blessed Him

"For this Melchizedek, king of Salem, priest of the Most High God, who met Abraham as he was returning from the slaughter of the kings and blessed him, to whom also Abraham apportioned a tenth part of all the spoils, was first of all, by the translation of his name, king of righteousness, and then also king of Salem, which is king of peace. Without father, without mother, without genealogy, having neither beginning of days nor end of life, but made like the Son of God, he remains a priest perpetually" (Heb. 7:1-3).

Blessed by the Greater

"Now observe how great this man was to whom Abraham, the patriarch, gave a tenth of the choicest spoils. And those indeed of the sons of Levi who receive the priest's office have commandment in the Law to collect a tenth from the people, that is, from their brethren, although these are descended from Abraham. But the one whose genealogy is not traced from them collected a tenth from Abraham and blessed the one who had the promises. But without any dispute the lesser is blessed by the greater. In this case mortal men receive tithes, but in that case one receives them, of whom it is witnessed that he lives on. And, so to speak, through Abraham even Levi, who received tithes, paid tithes, for he was still in the loins of his father when Melchizedek met him" (Heb. 7:4-10).

By Faith Isaac Blessed Jacob and Esau

"By faith Abraham, when he was tested, offered up Isaac, and he who had received the promises was offering up his only begotten son; it was he to whom it was said, 'IN ISAAC YOUR DESCENDANTS SHALL BE CALLED.' He considered that God is able to raise people even from the dead, from which he also received him back as a type. By faith Isaac blessed Jacob and Esau, even regarding things to come. By faith Jacob, as he was dying, blessed each of the sons of Joseph, and worshiped, leaning on the top of his staff. By faith Joseph, when he was dying, made mention of the exodus of the sons of Israel, and gave orders concerning his bones" (Heb. 11:17-22).

IN THE BOOK OF JAMES

Blessed Is a Man Who Perseveres Under Trial

"Blessed is a man who perseveres under trial; for once he has been approved, he will receive the crown of life which the Lord has promised to those who love Him. Let no one say when he is tempted, 'I am being tempted by God'; for God cannot be tempted by evil, and He Himself does not tempt anyone. But each one is tempted when he is carried away and enticed by his own lust. Then when lust has conceived, it gives birth to sin; and when sin is accomplished, it brings forth death. Do not be deceived, my beloved brethren. Every good thing given and every perfect gift is from above, coming down from the Father of lights, with whom there is no variation or shifting shadow. In the exercise of His will He brought us forth by the word of truth, so that we would be a kind of first fruits among His creatures" (Jas. 1:12-18).

This Man Will Be Blessed in What He Does

"This you know, my beloved brethren. But everyone must be quick to hear, slow to speak and slow to anger; for the anger of man does not achieve the righteousness of God. Therefore, putting aside all filthiness and all that remains of wickedness, in humility receive the word implanted, which is able to save your souls. But prove yourselves doers of the word, and not merely hearers who delude themselves. For if anyone is a hearer of the word and not a doer, he is like a man who looks at his natural face in a mirror; for once he has looked at himself and gone away, he has immediately forgotten what kind of person he was. But one who looks intently at the perfect law, the law of liberty, and abides by it, not having become a forgetful hearer but an effectual doer, this man will be blessed in what he does" (Jas. 1:19-25).

We Count Those Blessed Who Endured

"Therefore be patient, brethren, until the coming of the Lord. The farmer waits for the precious produce of the soil, being patient about it, until it gets the early and late rains. You too be patient; strengthen your hearts, for the coming of the Lord is near. Do not complain, brethren, against one another, so that you yourselves may not be judged; behold, the Judge is standing right at the door. As an example, brethren, of suffering and patience, take the prophets who spoke in the name of the Lord. We count those blessed who endured. You have heard of the endurance of Job and have seen the outcome of the Lord's dealings, that the Lord is full of compassion and is merciful" (Jas. 5:7-11).

IN THE BOOK OF 1 PETER

Blessed Be the God and Father

"Blessed be the God and Father of our Lord Jesus Christ, who according to His great mercy has caused us to be born again to a living hope through the resurrection of Jesus Christ from the dead, to obtain an inheritance which is imperishable and undefiled and will not fade away, reserved in heaven for you, who are protected by the power of God through faith for a salvation ready to be revealed in the last time. In this you greatly rejoice, even though now for a little while, if necessary, you have been distressed by various trials, so that the proof of your faith, being more precious than gold which is perishable, even though tested by fire, may be found to result in praise and glory and honor at the revelation of Jesus Christ; and though you have not seen Him, you love Him, and though you do not see Him now, but believe in Him, you greatly rejoice with joy inexpressible and full of glory, obtaining as the outcome of your faith the salvation of your souls" (1Pe. 1:3-9).

If You Should Suffer for the Sake of Righteousness, You Are Blessed

"Who is there to harm you if you prove zealous for what is good? But even if you should suffer for the sake of righteousness, you are blessed. AND DO NOT FEAR THEIR INTIMIDATION, AND DO NOT BE TROUBLED, but sanctify Christ as Lord in your hearts, always being ready to make a defense to everyone who asks you to give an account for the hope that is in you, yet with gentleness and reverence; and keep a good conscience so that in the thing in which you are slandered, those who revile your good behavior in Christ will be put to shame. For it is better, if God should will it so, that you suffer for doing what is right rather than for doing what is wrong. For Christ also died for sins once for all, the just for the unjust, so that He might bring us to God, having been put to death in the flesh, but made alive in the spirit; in which also He went and made proclamation to the spirits now in prison, who once were disobedient, when the patience of God kept waiting in the days of Noah, during the construction of the ark, in which a few, that is, eight persons, were brought safely through the water. Corresponding to that, baptism now saves you—not the removal of dirt from the flesh, but an appeal to God for a good conscience—through the resurrection of Jesus Christ, who is at the right hand of God, having gone into heaven, after angels and authorities and powers had been subjected to Him" (1Pe. 3:13-22).

If You Are Reviled for the Name of Christ, You Are Blessed

"Beloved, do not be surprised at the fiery ordeal among you, which comes upon you for your testing, as though some strange thing were happening to you; but to the degree that you share the sufferings of Christ, keep on rejoicing, so that also at the revelation of His glory you may rejoice with exultation. If you are reviled for the name of Christ, you are blessed, because the Spirit of glory and of God rests on you. Make sure that none of you suffers as a murderer, or thief, or evildoer, or a troublesome meddler; but if anyone suffers as a

Christian, he is not to be ashamed, but is to glorify God in this name. For it is time for judgment to begin with the household of God; and if it begins with us first, what will be the outcome for those who do not obey the gospel of God? AND IF IT IS WITH DIFFICULTY THAT THE RIGHTEOUS IS SAVED, WHAT WILL BECOME OF THE GODLESS MAN AND THE SINNER? Therefore, those also who suffer according to the will of God shall entrust their souls to a faithful Creator in doing what is right" (1Pe. 4:12-19).

IN THE BOOK OF REVELATION

Blessed Is He Who Reads and Those Who Hear

"The Revelation of Jesus Christ, which God gave Him to show to His bond-servants, the things which must soon take place; and He sent and communicated it by His angel to His bond-servant John, who testified to the word of God and to the testimony of Jesus Christ, even to all that he saw. Blessed is he who reads and those who hear the words of the prophecy, and heed the things which are written in it; for the time is near" (Rev. 1:1-3).

Blessed Are the Dead Who Die in the Lord

"And I heard a voice from heaven, saying, 'Write, "Blessed are the dead who die in the Lord from now on!"' 'Yes,' says the Spirit, 'so that they may rest from their labors, for their deeds follow with them'" (Rev. 14:13).

Chapter Three

Blessed Is the One Who Stays Awake

"The sixth angel poured out his bowl on the great river, the Euphrates; and its water was dried up, so that the way would be prepared for the kings from the east. And I saw coming out of the mouth of the dragon and out of the mouth of the beast and out of the mouth of the false prophet, three unclean spirits like frogs; for they are spirits of demons, performing signs, which go out to the kings of the whole world, to gather them together for the war of the great day of God, the Almighty. ('Behold, I am coming like a thief. Blessed is the one who stays awake and keeps his clothes, so that he will not walk about naked and men will not see his shame.') And they gathered them together to the place which in Hebrew is called Har-Magedon" (Rev. 16:12-16).

Blessed Are Those Who Are Invited

"Then he said to me, 'Write, "Blessed are those who are invited to the marriage supper of the Lamb."' And he said to me, 'These are true words of God.' Then I fell at his feet to worship him. But he said to me, 'Do not do that; I am a fellow servant of yours and your brethren who hold the testimony of Jesus; worship God. For the testimony of Jesus is the spirit of prophecy'" (Rev. 19:9-10).

Blessed and Holy

"Then I saw thrones, and they sat on them, and judgment was given to them. And I saw the souls of those who had been beheaded because of their testimony of Jesus and because of the word of God, and those who had not worshiped the beast or his image, and had not received the mark on their forehead and on their hand; and they came to life and reigned with Christ for a thousand years. The rest of the dead did not come to life until the thousand years were completed. This is the first resurrection. Blessed and holy is the one who has a part in the first resurrection; over these the second death has no power, but they will be priests of God and of Christ and will reign with Him for a thousand years" (Rev. 20:4-6).

Blessed Is He Who Heeds

"And behold, I am coming quickly. Blessed is he who heeds the words of the prophecy of this book" (Rev. 22:7).

Blessed Are Those Who Wash Their Robes

"Blessed are those who wash their robes, so that they may have the right to the tree of life, and may enter by the gates into the city. Outside are the dogs and the sorcerers and the immoral persons and the murderers and the idolaters, and everyone who loves and practices lying" (Rev. 22:14-15).

DAILY FAITH CONFESSIONS

(These are not direct quotations from the Bible but are paraphrased confessions based on scripture.)
SAY THEM OUT LOUD.

I am God's child (Jn. 1:12). I am royalty (1 Pet. 2:9). I am hidden with Christ in God (Col. 3:3). I am united with the Lord (1 Cor. 6:17). I am a friend of Christ (Jn. 15:15). I am raised up with Him, and seated with Him in heavenly places in Christ Jesus (Eph. 2:6). I was bought with a price (1 Cor. 6:19-20). I am blessed when I come in, and blessed shall I be when I go out (Deut. 28:6). I am a personal witness of Christ (Acts 1:8). I am a saint who prays in the Holy Spirit to keep myself in the love of God (Jude 1:20-21). I draw near with confidence to the throne of grace (Heb. 4:16). I have been adopted by the Father (Eph. 1:5). I am the salt and light of the earth (Mt. 5:13). I am the head and not the tail, and I am above, and not underneath (Deut. 28:13). I have authority to trample serpents and scorpions and over all the power of the enemy (Lk. 10:19). I am a member of the body of Christ (1 Cor. 12:27). God blessed me to be fruitful, and multiply, and replenish the earth, and subdue it: and have dominion (Gen. 1:28). I cannot be separated from God's love (Ro. 8:39). The good work God has begun in me will be perfected (Phil. 1:5). I can do all things through Christ who strengthens me (Phil. 4:13). No weapon that is formed against me will prosper (Is. 54:17). So then faith cometh by hearing, and hearing by the word of God (Ro. 10:17 KJV). Faith is my currency to operate in the kingdom of God (Ro. 14:23). I am God's workmanship created in Christ Jesus for good works, which God prepared beforehand (Eph. 2:10). I have been appointed to bear fruit, and that my fruit would remain (Jn. 15:16). I am being wise when I am winning souls for King Jesus (Pr. 11:30). My body is the temple of the Holy Spirit (1 Cor. 6:19). I have access to God through the Holy Spirit (Eph. 2:18). I have been justified (Ro. 5:1). Therefore there is now no condemnation for those who are in Christ Jesus (Ro. 8:1). Greater is He who is in me than he who is in the world (1 Jn. 4:4). I will do greater works than Jesus because He went to the Father (Jn. 14:12). As God was with Moses, He will be with me; God will not fail me or forsake me (Jos. 1:5). I see myself the way God see me. God sees me as a king (Gen, 17:6, Rev. 1:6) God sees me as royalty (1 Pet. 2:9). God sees me as the righteousness of God in Christ, bold as a lion (Ro. 3:22, Pr. 28:1). God sees me without spot or wrinkle because of the blood of Jesus (1 Pet. 1:19). I am having faith for big things because God owns everything and I'm His son (Ps. 24:1). No man will be able to stand before me all the days of my life (Jos. 1:5). My Father is glorified by this that I bear much fruit, and proves I'm a disciple (see Jn. 15:8). I think big and confess big things because God is big (Ps. 24:1). I will respect God for the big God that He is and my mouth will create whatever I want (Lk. 6:45). I no longer think of millions, my renewed mind thinks of billions because the wealth of the wicked is laid up for the righteous (Pr. 13:22). The sinner's job is to gather and collect for the one who is good in God's sight (Ecc. 2:26). Redemption is not complete without prosperity. Jesus hung on the cross so I can have the whole package, not just salvation (2 Cor. 8:9). I don't have to qualify, Jesus has qualified me. Jesus reversed the curse. The devil is a liar, and Jesus is the Messiah. Jesus is made unto me wisdom, righteousness, sanctification, and redemption (1 Cor. 1:30). I submit to God, I resist the devil and he flees from me (Jas. 4:7). For God has not given me the spirit of fear; but of power, and of love, and of a sound mind (2 Tim. 1:7). The Holy Spirit will teach me all things (Jn. 14:26). The Holy Spirit will guide me into all truth (Jn.16:13). The Holy Spirit abides in me, and I don't need anyone to teach me, but the anointing teaches me all things (1 Jn. 2:27). I quench fiery darts from the wicked one with the shield of faith (Eph. 6:16). I stand firm against the schemes of the devil (Eph. 6:11). I already have the victory and Satan cannot back me up. I hold my position of consistent victory after victory (2 Cor. 2:14). I walk in love and live by faith (Gal. 5:6). I have been redeemed from the curse of the law, poverty, sickness, and spiritual death (Gal. 3:13; Deut. 28). I will bear so much fruit. I'm God's workmanship created beforehand for good works (Eph. 2:10). God's favor is on my life (Ps. 3:8). God blesses me and His favor surrounds me as with a shield (Ps. 5:12). The kingdom of God is within me (Lk. 17:21). I have a production plant inside of me that bears fruit to change the world (Gen. 1:28). God gives me power to get wealth to establish His covenant on earth (Deut. 8:18). I am blessed to be a blessing (Gen. 12:2). I have Satan on the run. I will make a mockery of him (Jas. 4:7). I'm spending forever with King Jesus (2 Cor. 5:8)!

PRAYER FOR SALVATION

Say the following prayer out loud.

Heavenly Father, I am a sinner and I need a Savior. I confess Jesus Christ as the Lord of my life. I repent of all my sins. Father, I truly believe you raised Jesus from the dead. I pray this prayer in Jesus' name. Father, I am your child because Jesus is my Lord. I want to receive the fullness of the Holy Spirit. Holy Spirit come into me and fill me so I can be a mighty witness for King Jesus. I pray this prayer in Jesus' name Amen.

ABOUT THE AUTHOR

Eugene Carvalho is the founder of Receiving by Faith. He is an administrator and Christian author of seventy books. God uses him in the offices of pastor, evangelist and prophet. He holds a bachelor's degree in biblical studies and a double minor in pastoral ministry and world missions. He also holds a master's degree in practical theology. Eugene prayed for a translator and God sent his wife Mercedes who has a six-year degree in Spanish from a university in Tampico, Mexico. They have participated in evangelism in the streets of Mexico for many years. They have also traveled to churches all over the United States and Mexico winning souls and preaching faith. Their current ministry website is: www.receivingbyfaith.org

BOOKS BY EUGENE IN ENGLISH

To purchase other books by Eugene Carvalho visit receivingbyfaith.org or amazon.com.

Receiving by Faith
Faith for Every Day: 365 Daily Devotions
Faith Cometh by Hearing, and Hearing by the Word of God
Faith, Hope, and Love
Walk in Love and Live by Faith
Topical Christian Handbook and Scripture Guide
The Gospel Is the Power of God unto Salvation
Seed Time and Harvest Time
Your New Identity in Christ
The Cross and the Blood
The Holy Spirit
The Attributes of God
The Favor of God
The Glory of God
The Grace of God
The Power of God
The Promises of God
The Throne of God
The New Testament Church: A Survey from the Book of Ephesians
Vengeance and Recompense
God's Angel's
Prayer and Fasting
God's Mighty Prophets
A Survey of Jesus Through the Epistles
The Names of Jesus
The Psalms of David

Old Testament Miracles
New Testament Miracles
Mountain Moving Confessions
Visions and Dreams
Blessed Beyond Measure
The Righteous Will Flourish like The Palm Tree
Christ Heals: What the Bible Has to Say
My Peace I Give to You
Balancing Grace and Truth
Praise and Worship Changes Everything
Understanding the Importance of Authority
If You Are Willing and Obedient
Have Life More Abundantly
Sing Unto the Lord a New Song
The Power of the Tongue
The Supernatural: What the Bible Has to Say
The Truth Will Make You Free
Joy in the Holy Ghost
Praise Is Powerful: What the Bible Has to Say
Stewardship Regarding Our Finances
Love, Joy, and Peace Are Fruit of the Holy Ghost
Oh, Give Thanks to the Lord for He Is Good
The Kingdom of Heaven is at Hand
Acquiring Wisdom Is Vital
Grace and Mercy: What the Bible Has to Say
God Is Faithful: What the Bible Has to Say
God Is Love: What the Bible Has to Say
The God of Hope: What the Bible Has to Say
Pearls of Wisdom and Gems of Knowledge
Regarding Christianity
Victory is Mine, Joy is Mine, Peace Is Mine: I Told
Satan to Get Thee Behind
The Master's Gems
Striving Toward Perfection

For the Kingdom of God Is Righteousness, Peace and
Joy in the Holy Ghost
Encountering Proverbs, Ecclesiastes, and Song of
Solomon Through a Topical Survey
God's Feasts and Festivals
Speaking the Truth in Love
Spiritual Formation: Unleashing the Kingdom of
God within You
Prayer and Praise: The Big Artillery
Apostles and Prophets: The Foundation of the
Church
Be Strong and Courageous
Covenant: A Concise Survey
Sow Then Reap a Harvest
Your Word Is a Lamp to Me Feet
Prayer Is Powerful: What the Bible Has to Say
My People Are Destroyed By Lack of Knowledge
God Deserves Pure Worship
The Lord Requires Integrity: The Major Element of
Leadership
A Topical Look at the Book of Deuteronomy
A Topical Look at the Book of Psalms
A Topical Look at the Book of Proverbs
A Topical Look at the Book of Isaiah
A Topical Look at the Book of John
A Topical Look at the Book of Hebrews
A Topical Look at the Book of Revelation

BOOKS BY EUGENE IN SPANISH

Las Promesas de Dios
Los Salmos de David
Lo Sobrenatural: Lo que la Bíblia Tiene que Decir
Una Mirada Topica Del Libro De Los Salmos
Dios es Amor: Lo que la Biblia Tiene que Decir
La Adquisición de la Sabiduría es Vital: Lo que la Biblia Tiene que Decir

NOTES

NOTES

<u>NOTES</u>